CW00481126

# Human-Canine
# Emotive Energy Balancing

Communicating & Teaching with Energy Awareness

By

Janeen Warman
&
Meesh Masters

## COPYRIGHT NOTICE

Cover Picture courtesy of Lorraine Mallett Photography (Edited by Erron Silvester)

## DISCLAIMER

When working with, teaching and interacting with dogs, there is always going to be an element of the unknown. Everything we have written in this book has been taken from actual activities and exercises we undertake with clients, that have had very positive results on both behaviour and relationships.

Every care has been taken to fully explain and detail all the activities, techniques and methods we use, but of course, it isn't possible for us to guarantee success when we are conveying the information via just written words. As we cannot be there to watch and help you as you work through these techniques, we do hope you will reach out to us if you experience any difficulties, so we may be able to offer any assistance we can.

Nothing we have included in this book should cause your dog to become stressed, upset, anxious, worried or aggressive. If you notice any of these behaviours during your application of these exercises, or your dog has any pre-existing issues that cause them to be reactive or aggressive in any way, we recommend you consult with a qualified positive, reward focused professional to help you determine the best way to progress with your particular dog alongside the Emotive Energy Balancing techniques.

If you need help to find a suitably qualified professional who only teaches using positive and reward based techniques in your area, please take a look at the resources section at the back of this book, or get in touch and we will help you in any way we can.

# TABLE OF CONTENTS

# ACKNOWLEDGEMENTS

We would like to express our deepest gratitude to so many people for their advice, support and encouragement leading up to and during the creation of this book.

With special thanks to Kim Turner for her time and patience, for listening, prompting and finally providing the advice that was quite literally the turning point that gave birth to the idea and led to the development of the book you are reading today.

We are also very grateful to Karen Kay who has been in the background inspiring Janeen to embrace her personal development for over 10 years.

We would also like to thank Carole Hall who has been incredibly supportive and helped us with proof reading and editing the book and to Lorraine Mallett Photography for allowing us to use the beautiful cover image of Harris on the book. We would also like to thank Janeen's niece, Erron Silvester, for her beautiful edit of the cover photograph capturing just the kind of image we wanted.

Our expressions of gratitude wouldn't be complete without acknowledging our appreciation to all the great trainers, behaviourists and canine professionals that have inspired us and provided us with the benefit of their knowledge and experience on our journey as canine professionals. The likes of Dr Ian Dunbar, Sarah Fisher, Patricia McConnell, Suzanne Clothier, Grisha Stewart and Victoria Stillwell to name but a few.

Our final acknowledgement has to go to all of the dogs we've both had the pleasure of living with and working with. The dogs that have taught us so much, been patient with us while we learn and continue to inspire, educate and motivate us to be the best that we can be but at the same time remind us to keep it simple and live in the moment.

# INTRODUCTION

*"Your dog is a living, feeling emotional being,
just like you, but different." Meesh Masters*

Why did we decide to write this book?...

As teachers and consultants to pet dog guardians and their canine family members, our focus is very much on helping clients to live a harmonious lifestyle with their dogs, not just 'train' them or 'fix' that problem. We find most people don't want an impressively well trained dog that will do a 30 minute sit/stay or walk glued to their leg gazing up into their eyes, but instead really just want that easy flowing relationship that means they can go about their everyday lifestyles together, without too many major problems.

What we have also found, is that a lot of our teaching involves not only showing clients how to achieve the harmonious relationship they desire but is also about developing confidence in both sides of the partnership, so that our clients feel empowered in their abilities to achieve the outcomes they want, even when we are not with them. At the same time, in doing this, we noticed a reduction in anxiety-based behaviours in their dogs, they learnt better, faster and had more fun doing it, and there seemed a deeper connection between dog and guardian.

The techniques described in this book, are what we use on a daily basis when working with our clients and, as they say, the proof is in the pudding. We regularly see visible changes in both dogs and guardians as these techniques are learnt and practised. A common reaction from our clients is 'Whoa, that was awesome, he/she's never done that before!' Which, of course, is what we love most about our work!

We would like to take a moment here to clarify that the information, explanations and techniques described in this book, bear no resemblance to, or connection with, the phrase 'Calm Assertive Energy' as popularised by some dog training programmes aired on television in previous years. Emotive

Energy Balancing is a relationship development technique that we use alongside fear free, positive science based teaching methods, not in place of.

We have tried to make sure our book is easy to read, with lots of real life analogies that we hope will help you gain a better understanding of how intricately your behaviours and emotions are entwined with your dogs. We hope to help you see more clearly the world from your Dog's point of view, which in turn makes these techniques easier to apply in normal day to day life, both at home and on walks.

Of course, the techniques in this book are not a be all and end all teaching method but are merely something we have found to be highly effective, very enlightening and uplifting for both our human and canine clients. The aim of Emotive Energy Balancing is to approach 'dog training' not just based on teaching or changing your dog's behaviours, but by treating you both as one whole, unified symbiotic relationship, using human psychology as well as canine psychology to create a harmonious partnership that works.

We would, of course, encourage you to seek out further reading material in addition to this if you have specific behavioural issues you're dealing with, and to seek the help of a suitably qualified fear free training professional if necessary. There are many amazing trainers and behaviourists that we are lucky to have access to via the internet and printed publications, but as I'm sure you're aware, not all the information you come across is accurate and based on the latest scientific research and proven reward based teaching techniques.

With this in mind we have included a resource section at the end of this book, to help guide you to more of the kind of information we would recommend should you need it.

We hope that you enjoy the information and techniques we share with you here, and we look forward to connecting with you further via the various mediums we will be setting in motion to compliment this book.

## WHAT IS EMOTIVE ENERGY BALANCING
## & WHY IS IT USEFUL TO KNOW

Imagine for a moment, you're about 9 or 10 years old, you've just come home from school, and you walk into your house. There are no sounds, no one is talking, but as you enter the kitchen where your Mum and Dad are preparing dinner, you know immediately something is up. They both smile at you, say 'Hi sweetie how was your day' as they go about making dinner in the same way they always do, but something is different.

What is it?

It's their emotional energy. Unbeknownst to you, just a few minutes before you arrived home, they were having quite a heated disagreement about something, as sometimes happens in life and relationships. They stopped immediately they heard you arrive not wishing to argue in front of you, but you can still feel their negative energy surrounding them in that room. If you could physically see that energy, it would probably fill the entire room, like a mist or fog, but just because it's not visible to the naked eye, doesn't make it any less real.

Can you think back to times in your life when you have experienced that negative energy coming from someone? Can you remember what it felt like? It may have been someone who was angry, but it could also have been from someone who was feeling frustrated, impatient, jealous or shut down. I'm going to guess if we asked you to describe it, you might use words such as uncomfortable, closed, barrier, pushing away, blocking, dark, unwelcoming.

By the same token, take a moment now to think back to times in your life when someone around you has been ecstatically happy. Maybe they just got a job they really wanted or were getting married, or something wonderful happened to them. Can you remember what it felt like to be near that person? I'm going to guess if we asked you to describe what that scenario felt like, you might use words such as inviting, infectious, warm, light, attractive, engaging, uplifting.

- Brain Waves (thoughts) are a form of electromagnetic radiation = Energy
- Thoughts create Feelings
- Feelings produce chemical reactions that form Emotions
- E-Motion = Energy in motion
- Emotions impact on Behaviour
- Our Energy State is created by our Emotions
- We respond to the Energy States of others unconsciously

We are all affected by this energy, whether we're aware of it or not, and we have all experienced emotional energy transference, but most of the time we don't really pay it much attention or give it much thought. We may know why that person was ecstatically happy because they told us. We may know when someone is 'moody' or upset or anxious about something, and we can ask them and talk to them about it. So, although we are aware of the emotional energy, because we are able to communicate verbally with other human beings, we understand and behave accordingly in response to that verbal form of communication, based on the reasons behind the 'bad' or 'good' mood.

Our dogs, on the other hand, live almost continually by this energy. They feel it and respond to it instinctively, but without that capability for verbal communication, they have no idea why they are picking up this emotional charge from us.

By explaining how this happens and how we can use this information in our interactions with our dogs, hopefully in a way you find easy to understand and apply, we believe Emotive Energy Balancing is something that everyone could benefit from learning and practising within their day to day lives. It's not without its benefits within human-human relationships either!

Have you ever met someone or spent time with someone who you felt drained you? In psychology publications, these people have been termed as 'energy vampires' or 'energy suckers' because they quite literally drain your positive energy with their persistently negative energy. On the flip side of that, have you ever met someone you felt immediately drawn to? Maybe you never even spoke to them and yet you found being around them captivating, inspiring, motivating and uplifting because of the positive energy they emitted into the room.

Can you relate to both those experiences? Emotional energy can quite literally be repelling or inviting to those around you, but if you're not aware of it, and don't know how to do anything about it even if you are, it could be having some quite significant impacts on all your relationships.

So back to our dogs! As humans, we are thinking, feeling, emotional beings, and dogs are the same, but in a different way. Even though the way they experience and respond to the world around them is very different from the way we do, the emotional energy that can be transmitted between us is the same and plays a deeply integral and influential part of our relationship with them.

### In A Nutshell

So for the purposes of this particular book, Emotive Energy Balancing is the process by which we address and adjust the emotional energy between dogs and their guardians to help eliminate discord, improve communication between species and promote a deeper understanding on both sides. By working in this way, we are aiming to reduce stress, build confidence and enhance relationships so the life you share with your canine companion is the best that it can be for you both.

# PART 1
# HOW CAN EMOTIVE ENERGY BALANCING HELP YOU AS YOUR DOG'S GUARDIAN

*"It's Like Watching Two People That Have Lived Together For Years, Fall In Love All Over Again"*

## YOUR DOG IS YOUR MIRROR

Something we see very often when working with our clients, and in our own day to day lives, is a clear reflection of ourselves in our dogs. What we mean by this is, not just the fact that our dogs know when we're cross or sad, or when the guardian of a reactive dog has tensed up and passed that down the lead to their dog, we mean on a deeper everyday emotional level.

As previously mentioned, dogs live by energy much more so than we do, so it stands to reason they're going to be more tuned into this emotional frequency than we are at times. What's great about this, is not only can it help us to be better guardians and better teachers for our dogs but, in return, they can actually help us to become better people.

By learning how to become more aware of both our own and our dogs' emotional states, we can become skilled at changing our energy and subsequently our behaviour according to each situation, because our dogs don't have the mental capacity to be able to do this - they simply mirror back to us. This raw emotional feedback we get from our wonderful four-pawed friends means we are able to learn and practise how to avoid being governed by unchecked emotional reactions and, instead, be able to interrupt that previously subconscious process and change it for a better option.

We have probably all seen changes in our dogs behaviour when we are ill, stressed, happy, crying or any number of strong emotional states, now we want to help you build on that foundation, and learn the more subtle nuances of energy awareness, and how it can be mindfully channeled to have a positive impact on your dogs behaviour.

We have seen time and time again how the smallest changes can make big differences in the speed they learn at, the speed they progress at and, best of all, the profound change it can bring about in the relationship between the guardian and their dog.

In her book, Emotional Contagion (1994) author and social psychologist Elaine Hatfield defined primitive emotional contagion as:

> *The tendency to automatically mimic and synchronize facial expressions, vocalizations, postures, and movements with those of another person and, consequently, to converge emotionally. (Hatfield et al., 1992, pp. 153-154)*

In the Corsini Encyclopedia of Psychology & Behavioural Science, it states:

> *Researchers from a variety of disciplines have provided evidence that emotional contagion exists. The majority of such work has come from animal researchers (Miller, Banks. & Ogawa. 1963); child psychologists interested in primitive emotional contagion, empathy, and sympathy; clinicians exploring the process of transference and countertransference: Social psychologists (Hatfield et al. 1993) and historians.*

Whilst we have no desire to make this book overly scientific and difficult to read, we felt it important to mention that what we describe and apply in our Emotive Energy Balancing techniques, are our interpretations and applications of scientifically researched information that we use successfully in our interactions with both human and canine students.

## YOUR ROLE AS YOUR DOG'S GUARDIAN

Without wishing to open the can of worms that is anthropomorphism, there are many similarities that can be useful to draw upon from our human-human relationships and applied to our human-canine relationships.

Can you imagine a world where we didn't provide any boundaries for our children? Didn't teach them appropriate social behaviour, or how to stay safe out in the big wide world. If we didn't teach them right from wrong, gave in to their every demand, repeatedly rewarded their tantrums or ignored their fears and insecurities.

Just like children, your dog needs feedback, they need education, direction and they need your reassurance at times. They need to know when they're doing well, not just when they're getting things wrong, but remember their 'wrong' behaviour is only wrong according to humans. From the dog's point of view, there are no problem behaviours, only dog behaviours that are a problem to us, or inappropriate for the world they live in.

By providing consistent boundaries and direction for our dogs, we are able to minimise stress (which is often at the root of a dogs learning difficulties and behavioural problems) eliminate confusion, and be able to naturally promote steady energy states and the kinds of behaviours that we generally class as 'good' behaviours.

So if your dog constantly demands your attention, gets in your face, barks to get on your lap and you give in every time, chances are you could end up with a demanding canine that's used to getting their own way all the time, and this will transfer into other areas of day to day life as well. By the same token, if your dog relies on you too much for emotional support, needs to follow you everywhere, has no confidence or ability to relax by themselves, this too can be an unpleasant way for a dog to live on a daily basis.

Speaking of children, we felt it worth mentioning quickly here, that children's energy can have quite a significant impact on many dogs, especially breeds of a more sensitive or highly strung nature. A child's energy is often excitable, unpredictable, not under control, and can alter in an instant from calm and peaceful, to highly energized or even frenzied (you know those tantrums we mean!).

Many dogs can find these swift and extreme energy changes uncomfortable and confusing at times and don't know how to handle them, especially if they haven't been raised with children from a young age, but even those that have can find it difficult coping with them sometimes. This confusion can cause a dog to become stressed which, in turn, can have an impact on their behaviours, making them seem unpredictable or out of character. There are further details on this in the sections on Stress Stacking and Energy Management.

One thing we would encourage every family to do is teach their children and any children that come to visit, how to diffuse situations where dogs can become over-aroused, excessively excited or stressed. This usually manifests itself as jumping at children, nipping at them, mouthing at them, biting feet, chasing, barking and generally using children as chew toys. We explain how to do this in Part 3, and most children find this quite a fun exercise and enjoy being empowered with the ability to calm a dog down when they need to.

So with all of this in mind, part of our Emotive Energy Balancing approach is to look at the overall relationship between the entire family, both humans and canines, and we would encourage you to do the same. This is to make sure the best possible level of consistency, boundaries and feedback exists, making day to day interactions an easier process for everyone.

## BEING THE PARENT, GUARDIAN & TEACHER

Learning, understanding and applying the Emotive Energy Balancing techniques, can help dog guardians everywhere find it easier to be a better dog teacher alongside their roles of canine parent and protector. Have you ever been to a dog training class, or had a private training session with a local professional, and the moment they take the lead away from you, your dog is instantly transformed, as though they were suddenly 'trained?'

It happens to us a lot, and it's not because guardians are not effective dog teachers, it's more because, through years of learning and practise, we have a finely tuned way of communicating with dogs. When we apply the positive reward based teaching methods, alongside Emotive Energy Balancing, dogs generally understand more clearly what we're trying to 'say', whether it be with our words, our body language or our energies, and when you add all three together, it's like super quadruple HD to a dog. Everything becomes clearer to them, they understand, they 'get it' and all the guesswork and confusion drops away, leaving the path clear for concise two-way communication, and you can do this too, with our help.

The other cornerstone to the relationship between dogs and their guardians is for our dogs to feel confident that we are able to deal with anything they may perceive as a threat and keep them safe. If we can do this, then they will be more likely to accept the decisions we make and follow our requests in highly anxious and confusing situations, both inside and outside of the home. What we hope we have achieved in this book is to simplify the process of showing you how to create that level of trust, help you learn how to generate your own confident energy and ability to teach effectively with long lasting results.

## THE POWER OF SELF-REFLECTION

You may wonder what self-reflection has to with dogs and behaviour, but as we're hoping you're already coming to realise, much of what your dog does or does not do, is directly linked to what you do or do not do, and more importantly how your emotions and energy are reflected in your behaviours.

By encouraging guardians to take some time to regularly self-reflect, we have seen positive change in the areas of confidence, self-belief, motivation, focus and, subsequently, successful outcomes.

So how does self-reflection help you the dog guardian?

- It gives you the opportunity to notice negative patterns in your energy states and your dogs, and so be able to choose alternate approaches or responses.

- It encourages you to notice and appreciate any small changes or degrees of progress you have both made and also helps to prevent you getting sucked into the negative spiral of only ever focusing on the things that are still 'wrong'.
- It helps you become more aware of lifestyle and environmental stimulus that impact on your energy state.

By increasing your awareness of how these things affect you, it can help you to make small adjustments to either prevent them or alter any negative energy states they create. An example of this could be something like, on a Tuesday your boss always dumps a task on you last minute at work, causing you to become annoyed, stressed and frustrated. Being so close to the end of the day, you often arrive home in a bad mood or with a short fuse (negative energy state.)

By noticing this pattern you then realise, often on a Tuesday evening, your walks with your dog tend to be less relaxed than normal. Maybe you notice your dog becomes a bit more pully on the lead, or they're more reactive, or excitable, or more fearful than normal. Having become aware of the possible connection between this regular event that creates negative energy in you, you are able to be prepared and make adjustments to see what, if any, positive impact it has on your Tuesday evening walks.

So you can see how practising self-reflection on a regular basis can have a positive impact, not only on your ability to manipulate your own energy states, but how in doing so it could affect your dog's energy state too, which ultimately can make life more pleasant for you both, and have a knock on positive effect on learning and behaviour.

## AMYGDALA HIJACKING & STACKING

A brief dip into the science bit...

Is this a totally random subject without relevance? Well no it isn't, but why? And how does it apply to the human-canine relationship, teaching and solving behaviour problems?

Let's say for example you're not feeling very confident one day, or your dog may be nervous or seems to be more reactive than normal. Going for a walk is feeling like it could be an ordeal, so you pick a location that you hope will be quiet or isolated, but once there you find it unexpectedly busy with other walkers. At the first sight of other people, you begin stress stacking.

Stacking (sometimes referred to as an anxiety ladder) is something that both you and your dog may experience. Let's be honest we can all have those days, and feeling this way is nothing to be ashamed about.

So you think to yourself, 'Ok I'm here now, I've got this' then from out of nowhere another dog barks at yours, your dog lunges or spins and may bark back, this adds another block to your stack but you keep walking feeling a little jangled but determined.

Lots of little things continue to add to that stack, but it's not just you that's stacking, chances are your dog is feeling the same, emotions and energy are contagious, and even though you may consciously be trying to prevent transmitting your tension down the lead, the energy between you can be heightening anxious feelings for you both. Just as you think all is calm again, your dog innocently sniffs an off lead dog, that dog tucks its tail, cowers and scuttles forward, the other owner furiously demands you control your dog!

This is when your stack explodes and your Amygdala takes control. The Amygdala is the emotional part of your brain that regulates your fight or flight response, but it doesn't always respond rationally. It reacts to threats, which in reality are not usually life-threatening, but the rush of hormones this reaction creates overrides your thinking brain.

The dog walker you are now face to face with, has little or no real education on dog behaviour and is furious with you, telling you your dog is out of control and dangerous, and because you may not know as much as you would like to, you doubt yourself, and what happens is usually a rush of guilt, then anger, and confusion. You are almost certain your dog was not aggressive, but maybe you missed something. You don't understand why this person is reacting this way. Now when we say rush of emotions, we mean these thoughts and feelings literally fly in seconds through your mind creating anxiety and an overload in your brain.

And then it happens the hijack arrives, your rational thinking brain has packed up and gone. Maybe you shout, argue or cry, lose your temper and retaliate. You may do some or all of them in no particular order.

All you can think about is getting away, getting out of this situation because the other dog guardian now feels like a threat, upsetting you, causing you to feel ashamed and embarrassed, even though you're not sure you or your dog have actually done anything wrong, but you want as much distance between you as possible!

We've all had those experiences where, in the heat of the moment we do or say something that we later regret or don't understand. Our reaction flew out of us before we could catch it, and you wonder why on earth it happened that way, what were you thinking? Well, the truth is you weren't thinking, you were overwhelmed with an emotional reaction, you were hijacked by your Amygdala, which in truly dangerous situations is a life saving event, but often in everyday life, it can cause a few problems.

Well, interestingly enough, your dog feels the same about situations that upset them or overwhelm them. It has been found in animals that the Amygdala can respond to a perception in as little as twelve thousands of a second, they are finely tuned to be on the alert for anything that may hurt them or that could be a potential threat.

These things could be on walks or in the home and the outcome they want is the same, they also want distance or space, to figure out what is happening, and if they can't get it they may react or shut down. The reaction part is obvious to us, it's a very physical response, but when a dog shuts down we may not even notice, so if or when they do finally snap, bite or react, we believe it came out of nowhere which is usually not the case at all, we just didn't spot that they were stacking.

To be fair we're not always aware until after an event that we are stacking ourselves, so how can we minimize or stop Amygdala hijacks?

We simply stop! We stop and remove ourselves and take some time to rebalance, the importance of this is explained again in our reactive walking chapter.

By stopping and taking a moment to rebalance ourselves and our energy in order to get back to feeling calm and focused, rational thinking can return much quicker, but there are also steps we can take to avoid getting ourselves stacked up and ready to blow in the first place, and this is where focus is a keyword.

The techniques shown in part 3 of this book, will all help to minimize Amygdala hijacks for both you and your dog. You can work your way through them one by one, or you can pick the one you think will have the most positive impact on your particular situation right now and then come back to introduce the others. There is no right or wrong way to go about it, only what works best for you and your dog, and as you read through, it is likely some aspects will resonate with you more than others and we would say these might be a good place for you to start.

### In a Nutshell

Learning, understanding and applying Emotive Energy Balancing techniques alongside proven positive reward based teaching methods can provide you with the mental and physical skills to be able to feel calm, confident and in control of any situations you and your dog may encounter together, both at home and outside on walks.

## PART 2
# HOW CAN EMOTIVE ENERGY BALANCING
# HELP YOUR DOG

*"What You Do Speaks So Loudly,*
*That I Cannot Hear What You Say "*

As with humans, every dog is different, every dog has different needs outside of their basic needs of survival, and a different perspective on the world. This perspective can be influenced by age, health, genetics, life experiences, traumas (that you may or may not be aware of) and unintentional associations.

Conventional dog 'training' can, at times, suppress emotion in our dogs and this can cause further problems. If your dog is trying to communicate an emotional state and **your** response is incorrect (i.e. you discipline a growl or ignore a distance request signal) it can make the situation worse instead of better. When your dog growls, they are trying to communicate something to you, it's the only way they know how.

Of course, we fully appreciate that we need to do something about the situation, so our dogs are not growling at us, but we need to do it in a way that supports our dogs emotional needs, and enables us to address the cause of the growl, not just the growl itself, which is simply a form of communication.

The problem is, if you simply tell your dog off, or shout at them, yank them or smack them for growling, your dog may well respond by being quiet. You may think you have solved the problem, but what is more likely to have happened, is that you have simply **suppressed** the symptom of the problem (the growl) - your dogs underlying emotional state remains exactly the same, but now you have no outward behavioural sign of it, and no communication or warning of how your dog is feeling.

This can often be the scenario when we hear 'The dog bit someone for no reason, there was no warning' Sadly the dog is often then labelled 'Aggressive' and a whole range of potentially unpleasant outcomes can come about. Exclusion from the home, shut away alone much of the time, surrendered to a rescue shelter or euthanized.

Remember, energy states are fluid, both ours and our dogs, one moment we can be calm, but in an instant, we can become sad, angry, anxious, fearful, tense, aroused or excited in response to a trigger or situation. Energy states can also act like a filter on perceptions and interpretations: if you're feeling calm and in a positive energy state, things affect you less intensely than if you're in an anxious or fearful state, and again, this is also true for our dogs.

Practising Emotive Energy Balancing can help you to sympathetically approach both your needs and your dogs, in a fun encouraging way using a combination of practical reward based, positive teaching techniques, energy work and animal-assisted therapy methods. It also helps you to learn how to confidently respond to situations rather than simply reacting to them, through consistent practise, knowledge, confidence building and the development of habits.

For example, when your car skids on a wet road, you most likely react and hope for the best. However, if an experienced driving instructor took you to a circuit and taught you how to drive into a skid, over and over again for a few weeks, until it became second nature and habitual, then you would have the knowledge and memory muscle of how to respond when your car skids on the open road, giving you confidence in your abilities to handle such a situation should it ever arise.

For both people and dogs, when we **react**, there is no thought process and the reactions are instinctive, releasing contagious warning energies to those around us, causing a heightened atmosphere and mood. However, when we **respond**, we perform a practical learnt behaviour, fluently and with confidence, giving confidence to those around us including our dogs, thus creating a calmer energy around the whole situation.

So returning to our growly dog, by taking a moment to stop and acknowledge the symptom you are seeing (the growl) noting when it's happening, under what circumstances, in what environment and working to understand the emotional state behind it (the cause) instead of **reacting** to the growl, you are able to **respond** and address that underlying cause. By doing this you can work to change your dog's emotional state in whatever that particular situation was, thus preventing the growl from occurring in the first place, but not because you told them off and suppressed it, because you helped them feel differently about what was happening. A much better outcome for everyone don't you agree?

## IT'S NOT POSSIBLE TO 'TRAIN' YOUR DOG'S EMOTIONS... OR IS IT?

Conventional dog 'training' often focuses mainly on manipulating the external behaviours our dogs display in response to our cue words. If this is done by positive reward based trainers, they will do it by forming positive associations within our dog's mind of the behaviours we want them to do, and reinforcing them. The knock-on effect of which is a reduction of the behaviours we would rather they didn't do.

So, if a dog is in a sit, he cannot be jumping up. If a dog is focused on you, he cannot be focused on anything else. If a dog is walking nicely on a loose lead, he cannot be pulling on the lead at the same time.

That is, of course, a very simplistic way of describing it, we could launch into all sorts of information about classical and operant conditioning, positive reinforcement and negative punishment, but the main aim of this book is to explain the concepts of Emotive Energy Balancing to you, without blinding you with science.

So, is it possible to 'train' our dog's emotions? The way we see it, no, but kind of... let us explain.

If we look at it first from a human perspective, is it possible to train our own emotions?

Yes, it is possible, but in order to do so, you have to be aware of the emotion as it rises, interrupt it and be able to name it in order to choose differently with an opposite or alternative thought pattern (emotional response) which will counterbalance the original emotional response. This gives us the ability to handle difficult and powerful emotions without being hijacked by them.

With practise we can learn to have greater control over our energy states, whereas our dogs don't have that ability. So in order for us to be able to help them, we not only need to learn how to handle our own energy states but also how we can positively impact on theirs, to help them at times when they need it. Remember, we often respond to the states of others subconsciously, and so do our dogs, this is how we can help them.

Energy State Impacts on Perception > Perception Impacts on Emotion > Emotion Impacts on Behaviour

By being able to impact on your dog's energy state, you are able to influence their perception, which will help to alter the emotion, resulting in a different visible behaviour.

So as you read that, the answer to our first question becomes clearer, is it possible to 'train' our dog's emotions? Well obviously no, not in the way we can learn to train ours, because our dogs don't possess the same mental capacity to self-analyze that we do. However, as explained, it is possible, with Emotive Energy Balancing and the skills it provides, for us to help reduce the degree and intensity of our dog's emotional responses, so they are able to stay within a threshold that enables us to help them and teach them how to choose differently.

## STRESS, EUSTRESS & LEARNING
## TO MAINTAIN EQUILIBRIUM

As you learn and begin to apply Emotive Energy Balancing techniques, you should find it easier to start recognising the subtle signs and signals your dog gives to communicate when they are getting close to or exceeding their stress threshold or comfort zone. This, in turn, will help you learn how to easily make small adjustments to daily life as and when is necessary, helping to keep them balanced and in a relaxed and positive energy state. Each dog is very individual, so this is not a generic one size fits all 'your dog will do this', it's quite subjective to the personality of your dog and the lifestyle you live together.

That may sound like a lot of work, but actually, it isn't once you get the hang of it, no more than we habitually monitor and make small adjustments within our own lives, to help balance out the stresses of modern day living.

For the most part, people's lives nowadays are more stressful than they were say 20 or 30 years ago, and the same is also true for our dogs. The lifestyle our dogs live with us now is quite different to what it used to be, and this can take its toll, not only on our dogs but also on the relationship we have with them, which in addition can impact on their behaviour.

If you can imagine having a partner who just has no clue about your character, your personality, what makes you happy, sad, stressed or mad! Has no idea about the things you love to do, and the things you would rather not do, or how to respond to you in any of those situations with empathy, understanding and compromise. Do you think that would be a particularly enjoyable relationship to be in?

Unfortunately, this is the way many dogs live with their families. Now before you go getting upset that we are implying this is you, we most certainly are not! We are simply trying to paint a picture that will help you understand where we're coming from in relation to achieving that 'in tune' harmony that makes the relationship (and behaviour) flow effortlessly, because of the enhanced level of understanding our energy work can help to develop.

So, in contrast, if you imagine having a partner who is so in tune with your character, your intrinsic personality, what makes you happy, sad, angry or stressed, your emotions, moods and needs that they know exactly when to push you, comfort you, give you space or simply pour the wine! You will hopefully understand that this is what we're aiming for you to have with your dog.

There are many behaviours our dog's display, that are labelled as 'bad' or 'problem' behaviours, when in fact they are often stress or anxiety driven behaviours, and more often than you would think, fear driven behaviours. Many clients we work with, believe the actions of their dog are 'dominant' or 'aggressive' and are completely in shock when we tell them their dog is actually anxious or confused and sometimes afraid.

Many of the signs of stress we have listed below are perfectly normal doggie behaviours, but what's important is the context. For example, if your dog scratches a lot on a walk, they could be feeling anxious. Of course a dog scratching is not necessarily a sign of stress, dogs often scratch, but what's important to be aware of is the level of scratching and if that level increases at certain times or in certain situations.

**Some possible signs of stress to look out for:**

- Nervousness – easily startled
- Restlessness – unable to calm down
- Poor concentration
- Pulling on the lead / Biting the lead
- Refusal to take treats they would normally take at home
- Panting (especially if it's not hot)
- Lip Licking - especially if they're doing it when people or other dogs are approaching or close by
- Yawning  - When not tired
- Scratching
- Shaking (as if shaking off water)
- Destructive behaviours
- Excessive Barking
- Over-eating – pica (eating inedible things)
- Loss of Appetite
- Skin problems – Allergies

**Awareness Activity**

Can you imagine if every time you spoke or tried to convey information to the people around you they misunderstood or simply appeared to not even hear you?

We have found it can be an enlightening exercise to get our clients to set aside some time to watch their dogs closely, especially in possible situations that could be stressful, such as training classes, meeting another dog for the first time, strangers visiting the house, seeing another dog on the street and many other situations that we perceive as normal, but that our dogs can actually find stressful at times.

It can be even more helpful to take short bursts of video and watch them back, this gives you more time to really watch closely your dog's behaviour and communications.

If we can take a little time to learn to recognise when our dogs are feeling anxious or uncomfortable, we would be able to make sure our responses to their behaviours are appropriate for how they're feeling, meaning not only a happier, more relaxed dog, but also the prevention of further behavioural problems.

Acceptable levels of stress are present in a dog's life all the time, and are necessary to stimulate and encourage growth, but when these challenges become constant or unbearable, that's when stress becomes a problem, and the body reacts in a way that makes it difficult for your dog to cope with the experience.

As we have previously touched on, stress is also something that can build up and overlap into other areas (Stress Stacking). So, for instance, pulling on a lead is a stress-inducing behaviour which can raise a dog's reactivity level by default, this will make them more likely to react badly to any strange situation or experience that they feel uncomfortable with.

As with humans, each dog reacts to stress in different ways and at different levels. Something that may cause one dog to become stressed would not necessarily another, they each have their own stress threshold in every individual situation.

**What Can Cause a Dog To Become Stressed**
(Anxious Energy State)

Possible things that could elevate your dog's stress levels are many and varied, and as previously mentioned, are individual to each dog. Some may be obvious, but others not so much, here are a few examples:

- A change in routine
- Shouting
- Being hugged and kissed
- Being stared at
- Pulling on the lead
- Pain, illness and/or medication (e.g. steroids)
- Boredom
- Aggressive handling or training
- Training Classes
- Confusion (guardians not being consistent)
- Being left alone for too long, or too often
- An over stimulating environment
- Parties in the home - especially children's
- Dog parks
- Fetes, Country Fairs, Boot Fairs
- Long days out in new places
- Any strange situation or new environment the dog is not familiar with
- Strange people the dog is not familiar with
- Strange objects (Umbrellas, Balloons, a new ornament, a dumped bag on the street)
- Loud noises both in or outside the home - could include fireworks, sirens, workmen noise
- Travelling in the car
- Visiting the vets

Scientific studies in human physiology have proven that stress leads to health problems, makes us unbalanced, irritable, anxious or on edge, and it's the same for our dogs. Behaviours like aggression, destruction, excessive barking, over attachment and hyperactivity are all likely to have stress as a large part of their root cause, and these dogs are merely reacting to a situation in which they feel unable to cope or don't know what else to do.

Many people find these behaviours problematic to live with but try to solve them by working on the behaviour itself, rather than addressing the cause at its emotional level. So for a dog that barks excessively, yes you can work on teaching them to 'Shush' on cue, but if you don't resolve the emotion that drives the barking behaviour and creates the reactive energy state in the first place, your success is likely to be limited.

### An Explanation of Stress Stacking in Dogs and How You Can Help

There are two ways stress stacking can occur. It's not always about the negative things like being upset or scared, vet visits or loose dogs running up to your nervous dog, it can also be happy stress or excited stress. Good stress (eustress) and bad stress (distress) are opposite ends of the same line, so the physiological effect on your dog is similar in both cases.

Hopefully, the following description will give you a clearer idea of how stress stacking can happen, and how you can help prevent and manage it. As previously mentioned, all dogs have different stressors, and to varying degrees, and stress stacking can play a part in what does or doesn't affect your particular dog.

We always aim to place any dog we're working with on a stress scale, to make sure we are able to manipulate events and environments if necessary. Some dogs may be on a low-level stress scale, meaning their day to day energy state is generally relaxed, whether at home or on walks, they are quite confident characters and do not 'freak out' easily, and if they do, they recover quickly.

At the other end of the stress scale, we may work with a dog who is at the high-level end, meaning their general day to day energy state is already that of wariness or anxiousness, albeit not necessarily visible at all times. Generally speaking, if a dog is classed as being at the higher end of the stress scale, they will find a lot more things concerning, are going to reach reaction point quicker and take longer to recover from a stress overload. These dogs obviously need more assistance and management of their energy states to help lower them on a daily basis, thereby increasing that distance to overload state.

The example below gives you an idea of how stress levels can increase/decrease on a daily basis and is fairly typical of what would affect a dog that fits into the middle range of the stress scale. So, this is not a totally confident dog that would have a high stress threshold and remain fairly unfazed by most things, but at the same time, it is also not an overly anxious dog that would have a very low stress threshold.

The following example is based on the understanding that stress level 0 is a completely relaxed and calm energy state and stress level 10 is a dog's stress threshold point, the point at which they are likely to become reactive in some way.

DAY ONE: Starting stress level = 0

- Morning off lead walk = arousal +1
- Plumber visit = excitement/anxiety +2
- Afternoon street walk encountering cats = arousal +2
- Parcel delivery to the house = arousal +1
- Restful night's sleep = decompress and relax -3
- **Stress level at the end of day one = 3**

DAY TWO:

- Morning off lead walk encountering pheasants to chase = over arousal/excitement +3
- Afternoon field walk on lead = relaxing and quiet sniffy walk -2
- Restful night's sleep = decompress and relax -3

- **Stress level at the end of day two = 1**

DAY THREE:

- Morning street walk with cats, barking dogs and dustbin men = over arousal/excitement +4
- Friends round visiting = excitement +1
- Afternoon park walk on lead with off lead dog intrusion = arousal/reaction +3
- Restful night's sleep = decompress and relax -3
- **Stress level at the end of day three = 6**

DAY FOUR:

- Morning off lead walk = minimal arousal/excitement +1
- A long car journey to visit family = excitement +1
- A busy family visit with children and other dogs = much excitement/arousal +2
- A walk in a strange dog park with a lot of off lead dogs = excitement/stress/arousal +2

This dogs stress level has now exceeded a level 10 and they react with growling and snapping when another dog gets into their personal space at the park, which is not something they would normally do.

This is obviously quite a simplified explanation to hopefully show you the ebb and flow that stress levels can take. By understanding it better and knowing how to make tweaks and changes as necessary, we can help maintain and regulate stress for our dogs if they need us to.

Your dog is not able to manage their environment or many of the situations they find themselves in, and often these are the kind of everyday situations they have to learn to cope with. However, if you have a dog that tends to get stressed out, then it is your duty as their guardian to help them with that, to help manage their experiences, but also help them become more comfortable within these situations through teaching and behavioural modification.

Take a look below at the 2nd example, where we have made some small adjustments to the situations and environments, but those adjustments have helped to reduce this dogs stress levels, and therefore the likelihood of repeatedly exceeding their threshold and causing reactive outbursts or overload shut downs.

DAY ONE: Starting stress level = 0

- Morning off lead walk = arousal +1
- Plumber visit = excitement/anxiety +2
- Afternoon street walk encountering cats +2
- Parcel delivery to the house = arousal +1
- Restful night's sleep = decompress and relax -3
- **Stress level at the end of day one = 3**

DAY TWO:

- Morning off lead walk encountering pheasants to chase = over arousal/excitement +3
- Afternoon field walk on lead = relaxing and quiet sniffy walk -2
- Restful night's sleep = decompress and relax -3
- **Stress level at the end of day two = 1**

DAY THREE:

- Morning street walk encountering cats, barking dogs and dustbin men = over arousal/excitement +4
- Friends round visiting = excitement +1
- Afternoon field walk on lead somewhere known to be quiet = relaxing and sniffy -2
- Some evening brain teaser games to promote mental tiredness followed by a gentle massage -1
- Restful night's sleep = decompress and relax -3
- **Stress level at the end of day three = 0**

DAY FOUR:

- Morning off lead walk = minimal arousal/excitement +1
- A long car journey to visit family = excitement +1
- A busy family visit with children and other dogs = much excitement/arousal but regular time outs are included for rest and decompression with stuffed Kong's to promote relaxing chewing +1
- A walk in a strange dog park with a lot of off lead dogs = excitement/stress/arousal +2

As this dog is now only at a level 5 (instead of 12 as they were in the previous example) they may well cope with and enjoy this environment, but if it becomes too arousing or they show signs of stress, you could simply leave and go on a quiet street walk instead.

Reactivity has been prevented through the management of experiences and environment, ensuring down time when necessary.

The bottom line is, an overly stressed dog whose energy states are erratic, can be a danger to themselves and to others. On top of this, the increased potential for emotional reactive outbursts can create long term changes in behaviour both around the home and on walks. It's a sad fact that more dogs are euthanized because of behaviour problems, than because of illness.

So this is another area we encourage you to work on. We have seen significant changes in many of the dogs we have worked with within a very short space of time, which is testament to not only the fact that what we're doing works, but also that when our clients apply the techniques and methods that we help them to learn, they can clearly see the positive changes for themselves.

## DID YOU KNOW YOU COULD CHANGE YOUR DOG'S ENERGY STATE?

So now you understand that stress overload can be a result of both good and bad experiences and that energy states are very fluid and can slide in and out of positive and negative areas very quickly, you may be starting to understand why we wanted to share our Emotive Energy Balancing techniques with you, so you can learn how influential they can be for you and your dog.

As we mentioned in the introduction, an energy state is not just something within you, it is something that can be felt all around you, and our dogs are very in tune with this energy, which is great news for us! It means we can consciously help to influence our dog's energy state using our own.

Try it now (unless you feel it might upset your dog), without saying anything, suddenly start to act and feel excited, pretending to be in a 'happy, excited state' I'm pretty certain your dog's energy state will change as well. They may join in with you or wonder what on earth that crazy human is doing now, or their reaction could be a stress response to your sudden change in energy, but their energy state is likely to change in some way because your energy is infectious. Whereas, as a human, I could laugh at your crazy sudden excitement but choose not to rise and join in with it, our dogs are more instinctively affected.

So, being aware of this provides us with a hugely beneficial tool in our canine communication toolkit. By being able to help them calm down, or even become more excitable, we are naturally becoming more connected which helps immensely with the kinds of exercises many pet dog guardians struggle with, such as recall, barking, walking nicely on a lead and reactivity.

A mistake often made when trying to influence a dogs energy state, is failing to meet them on the level they are already at. It's quite an important part of the process to place yourself at the same level, but in a positive way, stream into your dog's energy level (this is explained more in different contexts throughout the book), then bring your dog down with you, or amp them up with you, rather than trying to get them to jump straight from one energy state instantly into a different one.

It is also worth mentioning again here, dogs can have different baseline energy states, just the same as people do. I'm sure we can all think of people who are naturally anxious a lot of the time, or naturally calm people, or naturally excitable people, and there are usually basic natural energy states for each of our dogs too. Of course these change throughout the course of a day, but there is usually an underlying natural state, that if you can learn to recognise will help you to help your dog more successfully.

I'm sure we've all met those dogs that it seems nothing could excite! Together with the ones we think might never take a breath and stop 'buzzing', and of course, each of these would benefit from a different approach in their handling and the way they are taught. If you work in an excitable energy state with a dog that has electric energy themselves, chances are you are going to struggle to make significant progress, in the same way, if you try to work with an anxious dog when you yourself are stressed, you may both struggle to concentrate and learn well together.

Energies work best when they complement each other and begin to stream together. Again, this may sound complicated, but actually it really isn't, and what's more, it's fun to do and amazing to watch in action! Details of how to achieve this are explained in more detail in Part 3, Techniques for Using Emotive Energy Balancing to Impact on Teaching, Behaviour and Relationships.

## PRE-EMPTING A CHAIN OF EVENTS

As already mentioned, we kind of owe it to our dogs to learn their language if they're going to be living alongside us as family members. Once we learn all the little signals they give us and their 'tells', it becomes easier to pre-empt and redirect, helping us to break habits they may have been self-reinforcing over a long period of time.

As dog teachers and Emotive Energy Balancing Practitioners, we hear your cries of 'But I don't have time! Please just fix it.' Our response to this will always be "Erm No" we don't have a magic wand or a secret drug. We will never judge you or make you feel like you can't do it for yourself, our goal is always empowerment, but you do need to understand that there is one way and only one way to change your dog's habits & behaviours, and that is with focus, work and repetition.

By paying attention to what your dog is trying to tell you, and using the tools we give you in this book alongside practical reward based positive teaching techniques, you could be pleasantly surprised at the changes you start noticing.

Yes, you could threaten your dog with aversion and force your energy on them, but this ultimately damages your relationship, prevents the flow of learning, can cause your dog to shut down, and rarely results in a happy, balanced, confident canine in the long term.

Is that really the kind of relationship you want?

Let's look at the human equivalent of potty training as an example. With human toddlers we choose a period of time when we are able to watch them like a hawk, paying attention to every movement, change in facial expression and acknowledge they usually need a wee after a nap or a snack. We wouldn't dream of shutting them in the toilet and hoping for the best that one, they go on the toilet and two that they would know they got it right when they managed to aim straight.

The same applies to puppies, you set them up for success by making sure you take them to toilet at the obvious times, after a nap, after dinner and during any extended playtimes when they might get so engrossed in their fun games, they forget they need a wee until it's too late and they need to go right NOW!

At all other times, you watch, you learn, you understand that when they circle in a certain way they need to go, and if they hide from you to go, you have to be honest and confess to maybe that one time you scolded them, and projected your negative energy at the situation without thinking when they accidentally dropped a poo on your pristine rug! Let's face it potty training for humans or pups never mixes well with rugs!

As your dog grows and develops their habits, you need to continue paying the same attention that you did when they were young, to pick up on the nuances (chains) that predict actions. That way you can become aware that your dog may tense slightly or heighten their posture rigidly, perk up their ears or even lower into a stalk stance before running at another dog or barking at the window etc. Then you are able to respond and rather than just say 'No' or 'Leave' in a warning tone of voice, you can become practised at altering the whole energy of the situation, by changing your own energy first. This can get your dog's instant attention in a positive way, and you are able to then distract and redirect them if necessary onto another activity.

Your energy should always be encouraging and positive, even if they're pushing you to the point of losing it if you can stay calm and learn to drop your energy in order to regain balance and teach, that will bring the most productive outcome to the situation.

If you are struggling to do that, which happens, we get it, then the best thing to do is stop and walk away, or stop and take a few moments in a safe area to breathe and calm down, so you can avoid projecting any major negativity into the situation. If the situation makes it impossible for you to stop or walk away, take a deep breath, and simply get yourselves out of the situation as quickly and calmly as possible to a place you can both take a break, remember your dog does not do any of this on purpose, they are simply dogs being dogs.

## MANIPULATING A CHAIN OF EVENTS

Here comes the Penn & Teller part where we share with you how we do the magic, or rather the part where we step in as mediator, guidance counsellor and interpreter to explain to your dog what it is you've been asking for.

Many habits have a pattern or sequence so there is a system that even the busiest of people can put into place. In this section, we are going to look at existing behaviour chains and explain how to teach a new chain as a method.

Each part of a new behaviour can be broken down into blocks, imagine the blocks they used to let you stack together in primary school, it's similar to that, and every new thing you teach can be included simply as part of your daily routine. Let's face it, if you thought that you had to find an hour or two every day to work with and teach your dog, it could be really draining, even for those who are motivated.

Luckily you don't have to do this, but you do need to be aware, present and focused until you reach a level that clearly shows, that both you and your dog, have become more connected, are communicating more effectively and getting progressively improving results.

This applies to each exercise or behaviour you're working on, and we recommend you try to focus on only one at a time. If you try to fix too many things at once, it is likely both you and your dog will become overwhelmed and confused, but you should find, as you start working on your energy balancing and becoming more aware of it, it starts to naturally have a positive knock-on effect in all sorts of different areas.

Firstly let's look at pre-empting again and use the example of a dog that charges towards other dogs barking at them, not necessarily with the intention of causing harm, as some dogs do it when they lack social skills, want the play to go their own way, have forgotten or never learnt any manners.

Every case, of course, is different, but in this particular hypothetical case, we are watching the dog closely, we then find their pattern and notice a few things, such as when they spot a potential play mate in the distance, their body lowers and they begin stalking, then at a certain point they rush forward barking. Once able to, they may try herding the other dog, or dashing in and bouncing out again, to forcefully encourage their new friend to join in. Unfortunately, the other dog could be stunned and slightly freaked out by this, and may well not appreciate the personal space invasion, nor want to interact.

If you think of each action displayed by your dog as a link in the chain, the actions that are repeatedly displayed every time before the barking starts, are the bits you need to pay attention to. Once your dog is barking, they are over the threshold and will struggle to focus or learn. By interrupting the chain prior to the barking, you can try to remove that particular block or link in the chain, to see if you can break the habitual behaviour.

In this dogs case, we eliminated the stalk by ensuring the dog's behaviour was managed on a lead or long line with another dog visible ahead. We then calmly approached the other dog, in a wide arched zig-zag fashion across the field, encouraging voluntary engagement activities (which had been previously taught) and this meant we were able to maintain a connected energy between us by encouraging our dogs focus to be on us and not just the other dog. This meant the energy stacking excitement was broken or interrupted and polite, calm introductions were able to be made.

Having broken the chain and maintained a relaxed energy state, would not only have had a positive impact on you and your dog, but also on the dog you are approaching, and this would have aided in diffusing any excessive energy spike between the two dogs. By reducing the energy spike, you help to lower the risk of any adverse reactions from either dog because a dog in a high energy state usually has a lower reactivity threshold, meaning it doesn't take much to cause a snap or automatic reaction. With this kind of approach, and with dogs being situational learners, you now have an opportunity to re-teach your dog how to socialise and greet appropriately.

The prime goal during this process is to retain relaxed, positive energy between dog and guardian throughout the approach, so a key factor in the success of the exercise is being able to adjust and alter your energy and behaviour if your dog disengages from you, which is why being present and aware is so important during the learning stages.

If at any point during the process barking had occurred, then the goal of the exercise changes and we need to regain a connection quickly by shifting our energy state to meet the needs of our dog at that moment. The exercises of 'Leave it' and 'Let's go' may have been appropriate here, alongside a shift in our energy, from one of calm and relaxed to one of slightly stronger and higher, but still positive inviting energy.

This shift in our energy can help us meet the dog at their level, interrupt the bark and successfully elicit a response that will enable us to regain their attention and manoeuvre out of the situation with as little manhandling as possible, which is obviously far better for everyone.

So as you can see, by understanding how chains of events link together and by learning how we can shift energy states to impact our dog's behaviour, alongside the use of reward based positive teaching techniques, it can make both handling situations, and re-educating within those situations easier for both our dogs and us.

You can find these chains of events present in all areas of teaching and behaviour modification and it can be well worth the exercise to stop and break things down this way if you find you are having difficulty achieving a successful outcome with something.

# PART 3
# TECHNIQUES FOR USING EMOTIVE ENERGY BALANCING TO IMPACT ON TEACHING, BEHAVIOUR & RELATIONSHIPS

## SETTING YOURSELF UP FOR SUCCESS

This section is to help you understand how to set yourself up for success when teaching your dog. What do you need to think about and how are you feeling about teaching? What is teaching and when does it occur?

The answer is teaching happens all the time, we need to realise that it happens within the tapestry of living with our dogs on an everyday basis, believe it or not, they're closely monitoring us all the time, reading every interaction and watching for those subtle signals that they live by. In much the same way our children learn our moods and can often pre-empt what we do next, our dogs are doing exactly the same thing, only they are much better at it!

They are also able to learn and respond to the context of our moods and emotions, they often know when they can push the boundaries a little and when we mean what we say. As an example when they are playing, we might half-heartedly say 'Ok Fido come, it's time to go', but without a great deal of conviction because we may be distracted by the view, or be enjoying watching them play, so they may look up, but then carry on with their game or investigating something intensely. Then we think, ok we really do have to go and give a more definite 'Fido, Let's go' as we turn to leave, and more often than not, if we have been consistent with our teaching process, our dogs will have learnt, at this point, they must begin to follow.

And this is great, for us personally, this is how a relationship works, I don't think any one of us wants to have a subservient little furry covered robot, that is too scared to relax in our company because we demand constant, immediate and complete compliance at all times.

We want our interactions with our dog to be fluid and flowing, with the ease of a relationship full of understanding on both sides. When you and your dog are connected and working together in unison, the movements and energy between you should ebb and flow, very much like dancing. So with this in mind would you step on to the dance floor and stand tense and rigid, order your partner around or push and pull them into position?... I'm going to say no.

What happens to us when we dance? Well firstly we relax, but then without thinking we empty our minds of anything else and we enjoy being in the moment, energy is flowing in rhythm from our bodies and we easily join energies with the people around us, in a mutual enjoyment of the music. None of us in this moment are thinking about the bills or the cranky car or a tetchy boss, we are simply moving and flowing.

So why not consider how you 'dance' with your dog, when you're at home if you're playing or learning something together and especially when you're out on walks. Are you relaxed, present in the moment, conscious of your energy? Maybe that all sounds a bit too much to achieve on a daily basis, but believe us when we say, with some practise and repetition, this could become as natural to you as blinking.

All too often when we are out walking we see people and their dogs literally walking along in different worlds, the guardian in their world, lost in their own thoughts, their dog disconnected from them, doing its own thing, until maybe the guardian shouts something. Maybe their dog responds, maybe they don't?

Whilst we're in no way implying you should be constantly doing something with your dog while out on a walk, that would be exhausting for you both! Our goal is for you each to develop that mutual awareness that connects you, even when you're not deliberately interacting with each other, much like two people deeply in love, at a party of some mutual friends, where they each know everyone there. They're not so needy and insecure that they move around the party constantly clinging to one another's hand, unable to go anywhere without the other, but each one always knows where the other is, and periodically their glances will meet across the room, each knowing they have complete freedom, and yet at the same time they are intrinsically connected.

## So Where Do You Begin

As Reiki masters as well as dog and people teachers, we highly recommend that you visit professional energy workers to help rid yourself of any blockages that may have been left by the general stresses of everyday life. We do however fully appreciate that this may not be something you feel the need to do, or possible for everyone to find time for, so there are some simple exercises you can do in preparation for focused teaching sessions with your dogs.

Chances are, if you have chosen to read this book, that you already have an affinity with your dog and you are probably also an empath, meaning you are aware of your dog's energy, and it matters to you how they feel and that they are happy. You want to do the right thing by understanding as much about them as you can and have the best life together.

However, there can be a downside to being a sensitive empath. Although we may be comfortable learning alongside our dogs in a private, unobtrusive and forgiving friendship, we can also be sensitive to negative energy as well as positive. Our energy can shrink if we come into contact with other guardians or trainers in a group environment or out on walks. You may feel crucified if your dog is 'letting you down' in the presence of other people, you may feel judged, intimidated or may even panic.

A good teacher will help you to overcome this, be totally non-judgmental and build your confidence as they help you step into the role of guiding guardian to your four-legged family member. In the meantime, we hope that many of the exercises here will help you begin to develop that inner confidence and empowerment for yourself.

## Own Your Space

Let's start with confidence. Firstly stand straight with your shoulders back your head high and own your space. Stand with your hands on your hips or hold your arms out and up above your head, the same way you see athletes celebrate when they win a race.

In her 2012 Edinburgh seminar, social psychologist Amy Cuddy explains how changing posture can literally impact on your testosterone and Cortisol levels, changing not only how you feel about yourself, but also how others perceive you. Hold what she calls a 'power pose' for a few minutes. Own your space and whenever you feel anxious or intimidated think of yourself in this pose before you shrink and allow your anxious energy to overpower you.

## Practise Self Awareness

Breath slowly and steadily in your pose, as you do this begin to concentrate and feel the energy running through your body. Be really aware of it as you work through the other exercises in this book, learning how to soften and drop energy, or raise it again, depending on what is needed in each moment and situation.

Although these exercises may seem insignificant, by practising them even just for a minute or two at a time, like a form of momentary presence, can really help them to become a more natural part of how you feel and move throughout your everyday life. In doing so, they become second nature and will become things you instinctively do whenever you need them, including when you are interacting with your dog, especially in unexpected or potentially tense situations.

### LEARNING TO SOFTEN & DROP ENERGY

This one will take a bit of practise so you can learn how it feels in the absence of any distractions, similar to how we teach our dogs. That way, as you are working through the exercises in this book, you will know exactly what we mean when we ask you to drop energy because you will have already practised and developed the muscle memory to do it naturally and subconsciously.

- Once again taking your power pose, but this time tense your body.
- As you do so imagine a ball of white energy just above your head like a crown.
- Now imagine this ball rolling down through your head then evenly dispersing downwards and outwards through your arms and your legs and through your feet into the ground.
- You should feel your body soften and feel a sense of calmness in your tummy.
- Tense again and repeat.
- Keep repeating this exercise until you can do it within seconds, without hardly any thought to it, and practise as you carry out everyday tasks or any time you feel tension in your body.

Why are we asking you to learn to energy drop?

With out of date dominance theory training methods, trainers would instinctively expand energy and use tension to energy block and force a dog into compliance. Sadly this way of training often included ignoring communications and calming signals our dogs would give us, resulting in relationship breakdown and emotional shut down in many cases. If you can imagine this kind of teaching from your dog's point of view, do you think it would be an enjoyable learning experience for them?

As we work through these exercises, especially those relevant to dealing with reactivity, we believe it is an important foundation of the teaching process to be able to help you understand how you can naturally prevent your dog reading your anxious energy, which in turn helps to influence their choices and reactions to things they experience. This is, of course, alongside learning and teaching your dog the strong life skills behaviours they need to live confidently and safely in a human world that is often confusing to them.

As we previously mentioned, one thing we would encourage every family to do, is teach their children and any children that come to visit, how to energy drop to diffuse situations where dogs can become over-aroused, excessively excited or stressed. By learning and practising this with your children, it can help them be able to calm your dog down, at least until you get there and can intervene. It can also be incredibly useful if your child is approached by a strange dog out in the streets and parks.

The technique for energy dropping is best explained to children by teaching them to 'Be a Tree', an activity developed by a wonderful organisation called Doggone Safe.

Teach your child to 'Be a Tree'

- Stop moving and stand still
- Fold your branches - Fold your arms and hands across your body
- Watch your roots grow- Look down at your firmly planted feet
- Count in your head until the dog goes away or help comes

The Doggone Safe website has many resources and information guides on their website pertaining to children and dogs and keeping everyone safe, so please do take a look when you have a moment.

SAFE ENERGY EXERCISE AT HOME

This exercise helps you bond and develop a mutual understanding with your dog.

- Begin by sitting with your dog and drop energy
- Then using the back of your hand hold it to your dog's nose the way you would if you were meeting for the first time. Using the back of your hand rather than your palm means you will not add as much pressure, making it a less invasive low energy exchange

- In sweeping motions, still only using the back of your hand, gently move along and up from under their chin, along the neck, sweeping into thin air at the shoulder.
- Continue sweeping over your dog's body, being aware of any signs of tension or movement away from your hand that your dog displays
- If this happens, move your hand away and back to a spot, such as under the chin or chest, that they are more comfortable with.
- Watch your dog as you do this and see if they are more relaxed with the contact in certain places more than others. Do they come closer and encourage the interaction between you? Or do they shift away at any point?
- Every dog is different and can be different on any given day, so trust your instincts. This exercise is simply about stopping and raising your awareness of how your dog may be feeling at any point in time and developing a more instinctive communication between the two of you using energy awareness, which in turn helps to build a trust bond.

As you walk around the house, you could also practise the flow between you, notice how if you turn sideways and sweep your arm to motion your dog beside you they are more likely to fall in. Move again encouraging them to stay beside you without having to force anything. When your dog becomes excitable during teaching sessions, practise energy dropping and low energy sweeping, then begin teaching again.

This section is to teach you about calming energy, but obviously, it wouldn't be fair to not allow your dog to have fun and enjoy some high energy sometimes. They learn so much through fun and play and there will be times we also want to raise our own energy and be more interesting and fun to be around.

The sections on strong energy, fun energy and energy matching and streaming should complement this section, as you learn to feel confident and trust your instincts on how to respond and connect with your dog in every situation.

## HAVE YOU HEARD OF POSITIVE BRAIN FOCUS & HOW IT CAN IMPACT YOUR ENERGY STATE

The following is an excerpt from Meesh Masters book *Teaching Dogs Practical Life Skills* that we wanted to include here being very relevant to Emotive Energy Balancing and how we can impact on not only our own energy states, but also those of our dogs.

So what are we talking about when we say positive brain focus? All this means is: It's more effective to teach a dog what you want them to do than to try and stop them doing something you don't want them to do.

Instead of trying to explain to your dog (which is very difficult because they don't speak our language) that you *don't* want them to bark, jump up, mouth, pull on the lead, run away etc. get it clear in your mind what you want them to do instead, and then focus on capturing and rewarding these positive actions.

Help your dog to find a Yessssss!

From The DOG's Point of View: Humans can understand when they're asked to stop doing something because words can be used to explain what we want them to stop doing. This is obviously not true for dogs.

When teaching our dogs new things, it's also easier for our brains to focus on and create a positive thought process (which promotes positive energy) like 'walk by my side' rather than a negative one like 'stop pulling', which tends to generate a feeling of negative energy and resistance even just thinking about it. Did you feel it?

Try it now...

*In your mind repeat the words 'Stop Pulling' and become aware of how those thoughts/words make you feel?*

*Now in your mind repeat the words 'Walk By My Side' and see if that feels any different?*

Did you feel any difference in how these words, even just as thoughts, impacted on your internal energy?

Even something as simple as this change in your energy by altering the way you think about something can make a difference to how comfortable your dog feels, whether they pull on the lead or not and how easy they will find it to learn.

## VISUALISATION FOR POSITIVE ENERGY

Another technique we actively promote as part of Emotive Energy Balancing is Visualisation for Positive Energy. When you repeatedly imagine you're performing a task, or behaving a certain way, or succeeding at doing something, your muscles contract as though you're actually doing it, and remember your brain is a muscle too. The contractions are so small, you can't feel them, but it's enough to strengthen your muscle memory, which in turn will help you carry out those actions naturally in real life.

Visualisation can be particularly helpful if you have something that you're really struggling to change.

Things like:

- You automatically tighten the lead when you see your dogs trigger coming toward you
- You automatically pull back if your dog pulls on the lead
- You automatically shout when your dog is barking like a crazy demon at the front door.

By visualising what you want to do differently, you can help speed up the time it takes you to change the automatic habits **you** have developed, which in turn can have a hugely positive effect on your dog's habitual behaviours.

Visualisation can also be really beneficial for building confidence in your own ability to achieve whatever your desired outcome is with your dog. Try it and see for yourself, but remember, as with anything, just doing it once won't make any difference, you need to do it regularly, say for example before every walk, but you only need to do it for a minute or two, breathe, drop your energy and visualise how you want things to be.

The following is an example of what a visualisation may look like for someone wanting to stop their dog from pulling on the lead, a very common and frustrating problem to solve for many pet dog guardians.

**Visualisation Example for Pulling on the Lead**

We are going to assume you have an understanding of the teaching techniques required for working with a dog that pulls on the lead, now all that remains is for you to visualise, apply and practise the techniques.

- Take a few moments just before you're about to prepare for your walk to sit quietly and visualise.
- Breathe deeply, drop your energy and relax.
- Close your eyes and see yourself and your dog calmly getting ready for your walk.
- Maybe you have a dog that goes crazy at walk times, so visualise yourself patiently waiting for them to drop their energy with you before you clip on their lead.
- Imagine you are both walking calmly to the front door, opening it and waiting for a check in from your dog, to establish that connection.
- Visualise yourselves leaving the house and beginning your walk, using the focus foundation technique.
- Feel how calm you are, smiling, relaxed and focused 100% on your dog, and how you are interacting together.
- See yourselves applying the lead techniques, see your dog responding, and becoming softer, enjoying the engagement between you.
- Feel your light, bouncy steps as you walk along together, connected by your energy, communicating almost as if by telepathy. Even when your dog starts to pull, you see yourself in your vision, without frustration, calmly stopping, using your body and energy to invite them back to your side,

setting off with a light, positive energy stride and rewarding them for staying with you, giving them constant, consistent feedback that this was exactly what you wanted.

- See how much more they seem to listen to you.
- Watch yourself complete your walk, seeing your dog getting better and better at learning to walk on a loose lead by your side the whole way round.
- See yourself as you both return home happy, relaxed and feeling accomplished.

This may seem like it would take as long as the walk itself, and it may take a little while to start with, but if you practised this kind of visualisation regularly (and regularly is a keyword) for whatever challenge you are facing, you will soon find this exercise can be done in just a minute or two.

## THE ENERGY AFFECT & EFFECT
## (ENERGY BUBBLES)

Returning to our explanation of what Emotive Energy Balancing is, the Energy Affect and Effect is something we work with very early on with our clients, to ensure they have a clear understanding of the simple power they have within them, that can profoundly affect all sorts of situations.

What we like to refer to as Energy Bubbles, can help a guardian to recognise immediately their own emotional state and how it is impacting on their dog and it's behaviour. By using the analogy of an energy bubble, like the negative energy in the little boy's kitchen that he felt the moment he walked in, it makes it easy for our clients to understand and apply this simple technique.

The Affect is how the Energy Bubble can 'influence'

The Effect is how the Energy Bubble can change the 'outcome'

For example, if you are in a cross or angry state, your energy bubble will most likely repel your dog away from you. This can often happen when a dog won't recall back to their guardian, so the guardian becomes more and more cross, but instead of this making their dog more likely to come back, it actually repels them away.

In this example, if you can recognise this instantly, and change your state to one of happy, soft or excited energy, along with inviting body language (turning sideways, bending at the knees, smiling, shuffling as if teasing your dog, moving away slightly to help draw your dog toward you) your dog is likely to find you immediately more appealing, want to come and 'join' your happy energy bubble and therefore choose to recall back to you, the most powerful word there being CHOOSE.

Another excellent example of how effective the energy bubble can be is when in tense situations. Perhaps you have a dog that is reactive when they see people or other dogs on a walk. We don't just mean when you transfer your tension down the lead to your dog, this tense energy is all around both of you, flowing back and forth between you, probably for most of the time you are on a walk. Remember, your dog is unable to consciously change their emotional state, and so will remain tense and on edge which, in turn, keeps them stuck in a highly reactive state.

A technique originally coined by renowned canine behaviourist William Campbell and often referred to and recommended by Veterinarian and Canine Trainer and Behaviourist Dr Ian Dunbar, is the Jolly Routine, and the Jolly Routine is a technique which relates excellently to what we are saying here.

The Jolly Routine is simply an instant shift in your energy state, whereby you literally become jolly, to influence your dog using energy transference in a potentially tense situation. This is a great example of using an energy bubble by first changing your emotional energy state, to impact on and alter your dog's emotional energy state.

A demonstration of the jolly routine might look like this:

- On a walk, you see an oncoming trigger in the distance.
- Often in this situation, your dog will tense at the sight of the trigger, and so will you (it may even be you first)

- So instead of simply continuing your walk toward the trigger, you change your energy state.
- You immediately loosen your muscle tone and body posture, drop your energy and become soft and wiggly.
- You might break into a happy song (this can be quiet, your dog will hear it.)
- You might start to skip along or walk in a silly way.
- You might engage your dogs focus and talk happily to them in a reassuring way.
- If you add in the rapid delivery of high-value treats as you move together, this can produce a double whammy of positivity into the situation.
- All of this makes it easier for you to remain connected and manoeuvre your dog away from the situation if necessary, rather than getting into a negative battle of wills or trying to drag them.

There will obviously be other things you need to do in this situation (which are covered more in our chapter on reactivity) but by first changing your energy state and so your dog's energy state, this makes everything else you need to do easier to handle and achieve. It can help you to remain calm and confident, it can help your dog remain able to respond to any further instructions you give, because instead of zoning out into 'threat alert' they remain engaged with you and connected to your positive energy.

It can also help to promote repeatedly positive associations with the sight of trigger experiences (scientifically known as counter-conditioning) instead of negative ones, whereby your dog ends up over threshold and reacting.

Some other examples of situations where awareness of your energy bubble can be effective are for things such as:-

- Jumping up
- Hyperactivity

- Lack of recall
- Mouthing
- Lack of impulse control
- Fearful behaviours
- Excessive Barking

## FOCUS FOUNDATION EXERCISE

Not all walks should lead somewhere. Many of us don't fully appreciate how overwhelmingly stimulating the world can be for our dogs, with all the sights, sounds and smells coming at them all at once. So why not turn them into an amble sometimes, **slow** everything right down, wander around just outside your own front door or in your own road, somewhere quiet out in the country or a quiet corner of the park. An opportunity to simply connect with your dog when out in the highly distracting world.

- Begin at home with the lead, ask for a sit and only put the lead on if your dog is calm, praise and appreciate that calmness.

- Then go to the front door. At the front door ask your dog to wait calmly, praise and give your dog feedback that they are doing awesome, but keeping it soft and relaxing.

- If you open the door slightly and your dog moves forward, gently start to push it closed again, repeat until your dog stays calmly waiting or sitting with the door open

- Once your dog gets better at this, and remains calm and engaged with you, you can start going through the door together, this is not about control, it's about staying connected.

NOTE: This has nothing to do with being 'pack leader' nor is there any dominance theory related reason for going through the doorway calmly. Pack theory and dominance theory are not something we follow or advocate. As we have mentioned before, teaching takes place in blocks and chains for both of you, so by creating quiet energy states and good manners at the door, you are creating a stable calm mindset within both of you, that will be essential in helping your dog focus and connect with you once you have left the house.

Ok so now you're out of the front door, do not be tempted to rush down the front path, take your time, praise your dog for looking at you (voluntary check in) and connecting. If your dog is lunging at the end of the lead simply stop (using slow stop lead technique) and quietly wait for them to check in with you, or sit and look back at you. Be really pleased, invite them with your energy and body language to return nearer to you before moving forward again. If they come right back to you, calmly give them praise and a gentle tickle before you move forward.

Continue walking slowly, stopping and starting, asking for waits, doing U-turns, asking for sits or high five's before you move off again, all as you take a stroll up and down your street or around your immediate neighbourhood. As your dog gets better and better at this, you can start to move more quickly and make this a more fun exercise, but to begin with, during the learning stage, keep it slow and calm, to avoid over arousal, excitement and, subsequently, frustration.

It is important to build these foundations between you in a low level distraction area, if your dog can't remain connected and engaged with you outside on one street, it's going to be even harder for them to do so in highly distracting environments, where there are lots of people and other dogs, traffic, bicycles, smells, squirrels, pheasants etc.

The added bonus is not only are you practising mindfulness and engagement between you, but you have also just achieved some amazing loose lead practise!

A human related example might be when a child learns to ride a bike and gain confidence outside on their own street, to begin with, you hold onto them, helping them balance. You go steady, and gradually build up before taking them to the park, and finally letting go. A similar principle applies to your dog as he or she learns to focus and respond to you in different situations.

Now you have practised the basics you are ready to move on to circle focus work. If your dog is reactive, it may benefit you to read the section on that before working on the focus foundation exercise and then combine the two.

## THE BONDING ENERGY CIRCLE

You may have noticed the mention of circle work and been wondering is this a magic circle? Is this circle for protection? In a way yes. Will it keep mean people away on walks? Well no, but remember when we told you about social confidence? It can definitely help with that type of thing.

What can you gain from using the circle? By working in the circle format you can achieve a mindfulness connection and just as importantly you polish off your loose lead walking, achieve an improved reliable recall and above all a trusting bond between you and your dog.

Take your mind back to that walk we mentioned in the previous section, the one where you had to deal with anxiety stacking. The chances are before you had even left your house you were thinking of possible situations you may find yourself in during your walk, and that could be part of the problem. When you're thinking about all this stuff prior to a walk, you're pre-empting things that haven't happened yet, and if like many of us you're really good at this thinking ahead thing, you will have been considering all the other dogs and guardians actions, feelings, thoughts and possible consequences as well. So let's just stop right there!

You're overwhelmed before you have even left the house and that is just mentally exhausting. Oblivious to you, your anxious energy bubble is likely to be having quite an impact on your dog, which in turn could automatically make them more alert to trouble. So we are going to give you a tool that enables you to stop thinking about how to react, and instead know how to respond if the need arises.

The basic teaching aspect of this is not new, all good trainers worth their salt know this stuff and so many of them are amazing. All we're going to do is apply it slightly differently to achieve a dual teaching method between you and your dog, where you BOTH benefit and feel more confident.

Our aim is to help you to stop worrying about what everybody else is doing, thinking or might do as you come across them on walks. There becomes no need to tighten up the lead and become tense, you can simply guide and glide your circle away from other people's circles, whilst staying relaxed and calm, safe in the knowledge that you are in complete control and confident of your abilities as a responsible, empathic guardian.

The circle is a visualisation technique that you can practise, firstly with no distractions and then slowly build up through low level distractions, into medium level distractions until eventually you're at high level like a pro and walking confidently in all situations.

So let's get started, you should have by now become really good at the energy drop and grounding, you should also have practised focus foundation with street walking. Now... imagine yourself as the central point of the circle, with shoulders back, visualise where you want the outside of your circle to finish. Usually, it is just before the point you know your dog is going to go deaf, and you will lose your connection with them. Keep your body free of tension and your energy gentle and calm.

Your aim is to keep your dog inside the circle using whichever positive happy method you have learnt. Having owned sighthounds and street dogs we really like 'Let's go' and/or 'This way' (see Part 5 for some instructions for these exercises) Stay relaxed and happy, add some bounce and enthusiasm but keep your energy and body supple, as you glide that circle around the field.

At first, your dog may not be in your circle, so walk in the other direction to them, as you call out '<Fido> Let's Go' in a light happy voice. Then as they run towards you, turn and face them but continue walking backwards and say 'come' ( or your chosen recall word) but say it in a way that lifts your energy, and in a way that says to your dog 'oh I've missed you so much! There you are!'

At this point, if you then ask for a sit, we might do something akin to a flying rugby tackle on you as the word 'Nooooo' comes from our mouth in slow motion! Because at this point, our primary focus is connecting your energies, we want your dog to feel nothing but happiness, pure joy and trust in that circle, we want you to be the best person **ever** to hang out with, and by asking for that sit when they get to you, implies simply coming to be with you wasn't enough.

When your dog arrives back with you, you have several options, and these will be dependent on your particular dog's motivators and perspective on what's rewarding to them.

- Have a little praise party!
- Raise your energy instantly, do a little happy dance, allow your dog to jump up at you and have a huge cuddle.
- Initiate an engaging game of on the spot chase.
- Give them major bum scratches (if they love that sort of thing?!)
- Simply do anything that really boosts the whole energy and fun aspect of being back with you!
- Have a little treat party! You could do Rapid Treat Delivery while giving lots of praise, which basically involves feeding a handful of treats quickly one after the other, so it's like a continuous stream of goodies.
- If it's safe to do so and there are no other dogs nearby, you could deliver a treat fountain, gently trickling a handful of treats out of your hand from above and just in front of your dog's nose, whilst giving lots of praise, so the yummy food literally rains down in front of them.
- Or you could have an instant mega 'Find it' game of scattered treats, so as your dog arrives, literally just scatter a handful of tasty treats all over the ground in front of him, as you deliver lots of praise, saying 'Find it, Find it' in a an

excited voice, as you happily help them rummage and snuffle the treats out, so you are kind of playing together. (They may need your help to point out to them any that they miss!)

- Have a Tug Party! If you have the kind of dog that loves a game of tug, then you could have a tug toy hidden about your person, and as they arrive back with you, you surprise them with the toy and a little game of tug, with lots of praise. It will help with this exercise if you can make sure your dog has a reliable release cue when playing tug, otherwise, the game could interrupt the overall flow of the Circle Exercise by going on for too long.

- We don't recommend playing any kind of ball or fetch games as a reward for this exercise because these games involve sending your dog away, far out of the circle, and what we're trying to establish is that connection to you, and remaining close. Certainly, these games can be incorporated later on when you have built up that bond, your dog's engagement and recall is spot on and you have that invisible connection that prevents problems arising.

Please don't be disheartened, if, on your first few attempts at this exercise, your dog follows but then flies straight past you and ahead. Think of it like fishing, relax and repeat. Repeat the turns in all directions, going in the opposite way to your dog.

If your dog's responses are initially poor, you can practise this first with them on a long lead or training line, removing it once they are responding better, BUT do not cheat and tug on the line to get your dog to respond. We want to know that they get it on their own by following your intention, words and actions. We want to make sure they're making a true choice in wanting to be a part of your strong positive energy circle.

If you have never done anything like this before, it may take up to 10 minutes of turning, walking in the opposite direction and zigzagging around the field or enclosure before you start seeing progress. If you are track walking going backwards and forwards works just as well.

NOTE: If your dog is not reliable off lead, is lacking any connection with you on walks, or your recall is very iffy, please be careful in the learning stages of this exercise and make sure you take any necessary management measures to prevent your dog from running off, or completely ignoring you while you are working to build engagement and connection.

So now that your dog is next to you, continue the turning saying 'with me', 'heel' or 'let's go' etc (whichever you find most natural to say) as they stay in step beside you. Be fun and happy, jog or even side skip as you encourage and invite the fluid dance-like movements of you both turning and walking in unison.

Practise and practise, and when you're confident you can get your dog back say 'go play' and release your dog out of the circle, and then follow them while they get the chance to do what they want, such as saying hello to a friend having a play or a good sniff around, we mustn't forget that it's also their chance for some canine enrichment.

While we are on the topic of canine enrichment, how does mindfulness and focusing on each other fulfill your dog's emotional wellbeing? Basically, your dog is totally dependent on you for stimulation. They only have the four walls of your house unless you take them out, they cannot come and go as they please when they get bored, they rely solely on the human they love to take them out. Quite often we are busy getting on with everyday life at home, so if we make sure that when we are out with our dogs, we take that time to give them 100% of our attention and focus, without thinking about anything else, then this is the highest reward we can give them, and it can also be pretty therapeutic for us too!

So as you can see, working in and focusing on the bonding energy circle can not only enhance your teaching success rate, it also helps both of you to relax, stay in the moment, alleviates stress and helps develop strong bonds between you.

## ENERGY MATCHING AND STREAMING

This is where we help you learn to validate a dog's excitement and vocalised warnings by guiding them back to a calm state rather than demanding it or stopping it with a verbal cue word and expecting an immediate response. In doing this, we can then teach them there are better ways to get our attention, and also that not all perceived threats are about to bring impending danger to the homestead, along with the fact that some perceived serial killers (in your dog's minds) are in fact quite nice people.

Imagine if, every time you spoke or had something to say, be it an opinion, expression or simply some positive or negative feedback, you were shut down and told to be quiet by your spouse, partner, children and friends, because they just didn't want to listen to you. They don't do it once but continuously over weeks and months, now I don't know about you, but I think we would be a bit bloody annoyed at first, but then we may become depressed or agitated, that the things we feel are important to voice keep getting shut down by our family and the friendship groups we are a part of.

This can be how it feels for our dogs on a daily basis when we don't pay attention to or listen to their various forms of communication, but instead simply keep trying to shut them up when they're barking, or shut down that communication when they're growling.

Let's face it, your dog has worked its fluffy backside off all day to save you from the big red serial killer that shoves things through your letterbox, the ginger sabre tooth tiger that lives next door and the pterodactyls in the garden. Have you been appreciative or shown an ounce of gratitude? Possibly not from your Dog's Point of View.

There are of course other scenario's where dogs bark, they can be demanding attention, trying to entice play or vocalising distress, and of course each situation needs to be dealt with slightly differently according to underlying reasons.

For now, let's take a look at alert barking and use the situation of the serial killer posting paper death threats through the door (postman for anyone that missed that.) Basically, when your dog barks at (what they see as) a perceived threat, or something they feel everybody should be aware of, your dog believes they are telling you 'Hey!! Human! There's someone there, look, danger, danger' because you are unaware of it and need to be told! If you don't listen, or try to shut them down for this notification, they continue to feel it is their job to make everyone aware this 'threat' is there again, and again, and again.

On top of this, because dogs learn by association and consequence, they believe their warning and reactive outburst made that monster go away, result! They don't understand that the serial killer was going to post and leave anyway.

In addition to this, the chances are, when they very first started doing this behaviour, you possibly shouted at them? This could have added to the negative energy surrounding the event in two ways.

1) Your dog could have perceived that you were shouting in agreement with them 'Yes! this person is a threat, we are going to shout with you!' or 2) The appearance of this person, who your dog already feels threatened by, gets **them** shouted at and told off whenever they turn up! Even more reason to bark harder and make them go away quicker! Either way, this promotes a very heightened negative energy around the whole situation, which perpetuates it and helps it to become a very strong habit (for you both).

The way Energy Matching and Energy Streaming works is by meeting your dog at the energy level they are at, but in a positive way, and then using your energy to bring them down from an excessive level, back to a manageable state. We do this naturally with people and children that can get excessively anxious about something, we connect and engage with them, all the while projecting our calmness and reassuring energy onto them, helping them to return to a more regulated emotional state. Obviously the biggest difference there is, we are able to verbally explain and talk to them at the same time, which, in any great depth we are unable to do with our dogs.

So how does it work? Let's say your dog is barking at the window constantly, you approach the window, with a slightly excited energy, maybe even saying 'Hey buddy, is there someone there' and stand next to them, taking a look to see what they're barking at. Acknowledge to them that you have heard their concern, and then thank them, seriously we mean it, actually say 'Hey, thank you, I can see it yes, that's ok' You may need to repeat this quite a few times in the early stages.

Remember this is probably a pretty strong habit by now, and is not going to turn around overnight, but the more you practise and as you both get better at this new approach to a previously very negative energy exchange, you should find your dog will start to calm down as soon as you arrive at the window with them.

Once you have acknowledged their concern, let them know you have seen the 'threat' and it's not a problem, you can then project your calm confidence about the situation, your energy stream can begin to reduce the intensity of their barking, helping them to return to a less intense emotional state. Firstly your dog is happy that you have paid attention and listened to them, and if you have shown them you have good thinking skills, they will happily let you take over and your energy will join together and begin streaming in unison.

Once this starts to happen, you are more likely to be able to ask for an alternative behaviour and actually get a response from your dog. You could say something like 'Ok that's fine, leave it now, let's go' (instructions for both of these cues are covered in Part 5) and because you will have previously taught these exercises in non-trigger situations, your dog knows them well, and so is able to respond. However, without this reduction in their energy level in the first instance, through energy matching and streaming, you would be highly unlikely to get any response from your dog while they are barking their heads off, no matter what you ask them to do, they are simply too absorbed in the situation.

So by acknowledging the threat, thanking them for letting you know, projecting your relaxed, positive energy into the situation, redirecting and maintaining your dog's focus throughout the awful letter posting experience, you can start to reverse this whole chain of events and break the habit, as your dog comes to realise that the person leaves the premises without them having to take action.

With consistent repetition, they will also hopefully realise there is actually no danger from this everyday occurrence, in fact when this person does appear, we are now building up a happy and positive association with the experience, through engagement with you, positive energy and being rewarded for maintaining a calm, relaxed state.

We do recommend there are two or three repeats of a verbal cue word to redirect or move away (leave it and let's go) as you leave the window because we do not want you to set up an accidental cue. For example, if you praise and reward 'leave it' immediately at the window, you could end up reinforcing the barking, and this could then become an even harder habit to break. So by creating a chain, even if it is two cue words repeated twice, and getting alternative behaviours from your dog that you can praise and reward, it can help avoid this happening.

Once you are more in sync with your dog's behaviour and energy levels and have a greater awareness of their feelings and body language, it becomes easier for you to pre-empt their next moves.

We do this with our toddlers, in fact without realising it we probably do it with everyone around us, because everyone gives a 'tell' the small movements that give a clue to what a person is about to do next. Our dogs see the world like this, so are better at reading us than we are them, but to be honest we expect them to learn our ways, so learning their expressions, 'tells' and different ways of communicating is the least we can do.

## COPING WITH STRONG ENERGY

We know that dogs thrive in a calm Zen-like energy zone, but in reality, the energy in our lives is not always gentle and smooth, we are not always in control, we can be impulsive at times and react, especially in an emergency. So how do we teach our dog that it's ok when we lose our shit around them (not at them) occasionally?

Just to clarify, we don't mean it's ok to be a neurotic unbalanced psycho, that's not healthy for any child, spouse or dog to live with. The cat's ok he can go out on the tiles, actually so can the husband.... but we digress! In all seriousness, we do not condone forceful, aversive, flooding, or scaring techniques when teaching or living with dogs, in any way whatsoever.

However, there are times in everyday life, that our energy goes off kilter, those of you with children know where we're coming from and it's normal, we do not live in Stepford, and we're all human beings and sometimes energy levels can rise in the home. Sometimes that strong energy may be aimed directly at our dogs, in an emergency situation, possibly life or death, so what's important here, is that we help our dogs learn to cope with these situations, by making sure they understand that strong energy does not mean bad things will happen to them.

As an example, if your dog has got loose and is about to run into the road and you have to act fast, your tone of voice will not be soft! You are highly likely to shout, and at the same time shift instantly into a highly anxious energy state which will project around you, but you **need** an immediate response to save your dog's life.

With a toddler, we may shout 'stop!' urgently and loudly and launch toward them grabbing them. Generally, a toddler will take a few seconds to register what is happening, which is enough time for you with your quicker reactions, to leap and grab them, but trust us when we say, this is not the same case when it happens with your dog.

The difference with your dog is, their instincts and response times are split seconds! On top of that, they will **instantly** react to your energy, sensing the panic warning you are emanating and may recoil away from you because of this, instead of toward you.

The trouble is, the way we react in this kind of real-life emergency situation is something that's very hard NOT to do, even if your dog already has a behaviour trained for such emergency's, the chances are when the poop is about to hit the fan, your natural reaction will be to shout and panic.

The problem with doing this to a dog is, if he or she panics with you at this explosion of tense, anxious and forceful energy that can actually push them away from you, it can push them straight into the path of danger. So we believe it's important to teach your dog, in a positive way, that a harsh tone and forceful energy is ok, and something they can respond to with trust.

With prolonged strong energy situations, such as problems at home between the human members of the family, we also need to be aware that our dogs can be affected. This can result in some changes in behaviour, and although separation into another room and the provision of a stuffed Kong or chew toy may help to keep them busy and provide a more positive association when important human issues are being discussed, it's by no means guaranteed to prevent a stress stack, so be aware that your dog is feeling everything.

So let's go back to the strong energy exercise, and those harsh, emergency tones.

- We recommend you only practise these exercises in a safe and secure area, so if your dog does disengage for any reason, they will be completely safe.

- We also recommend only very short bursts of these exercises to prevent pressure build-up for your dog, and if you notice at any point they are displaying signs of confusion or stress, end the exercise immediately and engage in some relaxing fun activity to help your dog recover quickly.

- If you're not sure how to read your dog, then please enlist the help of a positive reward based trainer to help you in the early stages to make sure you set yourselves up for success and your dog is happy working through this exercise.

- You could start by using a request your dog finds easy, such as sit and begin asking for it and rewarding them as you would normally

- Now begin to move around, requesting random sits in a gradually harsher tone, building up to the kind of strong panic voice you might use in an emergency, but in small increments. This should take place over many sessions to prevent stress build up and too much pressure for your dog .

- Please don't go from normal voice to shouting in one step, your dog will most likely not enjoy this at all and be unable to respond or learn effectively from the exercise.

- When your dog responds to your sit requests be instantly happy and soft again, make a big fuss and **jackpot** reward them.

- As you work through gradually building up the strong energy tone in your voice, as long as your dog is doing great, you can begin adding the physical aspect to the exercise.

- Repeat your strong energy sit request, and as you say it step towards your dog with a reasonably fast movement and touch the collar area, mark, treat and praise like you have never praised before. IMPORTANT NOTE: If your dog recoils away from your movement towards them, or it startles them in any way, make it a more gradual exercise, starting with a nice slow movement towards them and gradually making it faster as they get more comfortable and realise it comes with great prizes!

- Once your dog has happily responded repeatedly and is enjoying the fuss you can play high energy games then at random times shout SIT and be so happy and excited with the praise when your dog responds.

- Once practised and established with an easy request like Sit, you can then go on to add this strong energy exercise to other behaviour requests like Stay, Here (or your chosen recall word) Stop, Leave it and any other instructions that are likely to come to you automatically in a real emergency situation and are likely to create that strong energy response from you.

Even our nervous Romanian rescues respond well to this exercise when done in the right way, and the reason is because the energy, tone and movement in the exercise is built up very slowly at a pace they can handle and the payouts (rewards) are big and super high value (we are talking steak!).

You must be very conscious of how your dog is feeling during this exercise and proceed according to your particular dog and their character so to avoid scaring them. Not all dogs like energy bursts, even happy excited ones, so it is paramount that this exercise is done with care as it may when needed, save your dog's life in an emergency.

If you have multiple dogs, we recommend you work on this exercise with them individually first, so it is established and you know your dogs are comfortable with it. Once they are, you could create a group emergency response situation that you could practise at home first.

Say for example if they are all about to go on a whoopie round the garden, you can 'Stop' them with a strong energy request, and encourage nicer, calmer play before they annoy the neighbours too much! This can help you to develop a nice strong group calming energy exercise, especially useful if you have dogs that can get too hyped up together out on walks.

## REMEMBER THE FUN ENERGY

Why are we asking you to remember the fun? Throughout the book so far, we have spoken quite a bit about dropping energy, and how to lower and change your energy state to help calm your dog down, but there are also plenty of occasions when raising your energy and being fun can be incredibly useful, and not just when playing games with your dog.

When we teach 'Let's go' or 'Recall', 'Leave it' and Emergency 'Stop!' an injection of fun energy into the exercise, at just the right time can visibly boost your dog's speed of response, and can sometimes literally be the difference between them responding instantly, or not responding at all, something I think you'll agree is a pretty powerful thing to have in your energy toolkit.

We also want to encourage you, not just to incorporate fun energy into your teaching exercises, but also sometimes to just play games with your dog, with there being absolutely no reason for it and no outcome required. Just play for the sake of playing because this is such a great way to bond with your dog, and most dogs love to play in some form or other.

They relish that one on one fun time with you, just like our children do when we take time out of our busy days to just sit and colour with them, or play Lego or a board game (showing our ages now!) In fact most dogs need to play in some way, to feel enriched within their environment, remember they are living predominantly in one place, and are totally dependent on us to provide them with mental stimulation.

We hear a lot of clients say 'but my dog doesn't like toys, or doesn't like to play fetch', and whilst it's true, there are some dogs that don't like to play, what's important to remember is, play is a subjective thing. It's not just about playing with a ball or a game of tug, there are all sorts of ways you can play with your dog, and it may just be that you need to do some experimenting to find out what particular kind of play activities your dog prefers.

It might be chase games, nose games (scent work) problem-solving games, roll around the floor games, snuffling games or teaching exercises. Remember, if you're doing it right, even when you're doing 'training' and teaching your dog new things, it should be fun for you both, we all learn better when we're having fun right?

**Some Fun Game Ideas**

Hide and seek is a great place to start, even curling up in a ball covered in a blanket or hiding in a box can be fun, as your dog tries to get you out and see your face, this is a Nando Brown favourite and you can find many videos of him online hiding from his dog.

You could also try hiding treats around the house and play find it. To begin with place the treats and take your dog around the room pointing to each treat as they pick it up, excitedly saying 'find it, find it.' After a few goes you can start to hide the treats in more difficult places, then just say 'find it' and get excited with your dog every time they succeed in finding the treats all by themselves.

Dancing and being jolly, have you ever been really happy about something and danced around the room to find your dog joins you in celebrating, well do this just for the sheer hell of it and chances are your dog will love it!

Dr Ian Dunbar recommends a recall in the house game with two or more people: call your dog from different rooms, whoever the dog is with says 'find <name>' then that person calls, once the dog reaches that person celebrate! Then the next person hides and calls in the same way. Bonuses for this activity are fun recall repetition exercises, name recognition practise and physical exercise as well as mental stimulation. Once they get good at this then you could combine it with hide and seek.

Victoria Stillwell suggests a fun 'intention' experiment game in her online course 'Inside Your Dog's Mind'. Place two upside-down cups on the floor, let your dog see you place a treat, step back and point to the cup with the treat, your dog will learn to follow where you point and understand your intention. Try it out and then try pointing to the cup without the treat, your dog's trust in what you say may surprise you!

There are so many good trainers and good books with ideas on play and canine enrichment: teaching tricks can also be really good fun so look out for those books too. Basically, if you are both having great fun, then give it a go your dog will love it and love you for introducing it.

## ENERGY STACK MANAGEMENT

In much the same way as our dogs can stress stack because they are so strongly influenced by energy, it is also possible at times that they could 'energy stack' and being aware of this can help you understand what is happening and either make allowances or change something if necessary.

Energy stacking does not usually result in quite so extreme behaviour changes as stress stacking, but there can certainly be noticeable changes. So what kind of things can cause energy stacking, let's take a look at a few:

- More people in a room, at a house or on a walk (More people = more and varied energy)
- A new person joining you for a walk (especially if they have anxious/nervous energy)
- Children joining you for a walk when they don't normally (Children give off high energy vibes)
- Hyper play times, either with children or with adults (Everybody's energy is stacking!)
- Energising games such as extreme chase games or excessive ball throwing

Now let's take a quick look at the sorts of behavioural things you might see in a dog that is energy stacking:

- Lack of concentration on walks
- Less engagement with you and not listening to you as much as they normally would in the home or on walks (this can also be relevant to stress stacking)
- Appear to have forgotten things they normally do well. Not coming when called, won't sit or walk nicely on the lead when normally they would be able to do these things.
- Excessive excitement / Hyper behaviour

- A desire to take themselves off away from a situation (this could be at home or on walks)
- An increase in 'rude' behaviours such as jumping, mouthing, nipping or being destructive
- An inability to relax and calm down, pacing or being on high alert

For the most part, many of these things are not a major problem, and often once the circumstances have reverted back as they usually are, normal levels of service are resumed and your dog appears to have just been having a 'bad day'. This is of course entirely possible, but we felt it worth mentioning that it could also be to do with the degree of energy in the situation having an impact.

Being aware of this possibility enables you to either cut your dog some slack, preventing you from becoming frustrated or cross with them or take some measures to help your dog either deal with the energy stack or make some adjustments within the situation itself to help diffuse the energy stack for them.

## HELP YOUR DOG LEARN HOW TO DROP ENERGY AND RELAX

As previously mentioned, dogs are unable to process and analyse feelings the way we do, so how can we help them to know the beneficial ones from the destructive ones?

It's quite a simple, a common sense process and will help your dog learn to relax more and hopefully, in most cases, feel less anxiety. It should also help them to learn that they can leave you in charge of family protection duties, and a handy knock-on effect is that when you come to teach them new things in new places, the trust bond between you should be stronger, giving your dog the confidence to follow your lead.

The full step by step guide to teaching your dog to Self-Settle is explained in Part 5, but why bother teaching a dog to, in effect just lay down and relax? Many dogs develop, what we class as annoying or problem behaviours, because of anxiety, boredom or lack of interaction, all of which can manifest as a dog that becomes demanding, hyperactive, destructive, barks a lot, has no impulse control or literally never calms down!

We could, of course, try just ignoring them at these times, and yes, eventually ignoring them most of the time may work, but think about it from your dog's point of view. If you're only interacting with them (even if it's swearing under your breath) when they're fussing you, barking at you, jumping on you or destroying something, but then they don't receive any attention or feedback from you when they're behaving well or being good, how will they know what you want?

They will keep fussing to get a reaction from you or some kind of reassurance, or anything that lets them know you care. To them 'get lost Fido' is still a term of endearment when they have been ignored for a long period of time, which if you think about it, is quite sad.

I'm pretty sure none of us wants an anxious, depressed or lonely dog, so by doing the energy dropping self-relaxation exercises in Part 5, we can help our dogs learn that chilling out is a really good thing, we will still notice them and interact with them, and that there's no need to panic every time we leave the room or get out of our seat, we will come back.

## USING ENRICHMENT ACTIVITIES TO BUILD TRUST & PROMOTE SELF-RELAXATION AT HOME

You may already be aware of toy rotation (rotating toys can help stop boredom developing from having the same thing laying around constantly. It revives the interest, like oh haven't seen that for a while!) You may also have been told to save special toys for when you leave your dogs on their own, BUT consider this, if you suffered with anxiety and every time I left you I gave you a cheese sandwich, chances are you may not be able to face eating it, because you associate it with separation from people you love.

Although there are many different types of chews, enrichment and feeder toys available, we will just say Kong, for now, to make it less complicated.

The magic Kong is no different to that cheese sandwich. To help our dogs learn to energy drop and relax by themselves, we need to build an association of comfort, reassurance and sense of calm to the Kong. This can be done by doing the following trust-building exercise a few minutes a day (you can also apply the same principle if you're doing crate/den trust exercises).

To Begin Trust Building:

- Have a comfortable bed or mat for your dog near a seat that is comfortable for you to sit on. Give your dog their stuffed Kong/chew toy, drop your energy and sit quietly without talking
- If your dog moves then gently and quietly redirect them back onto the mat with the Kong.
- Repeat for just 5 or 10 minutes each day, standing up and sitting back down.
- This is essentially giving your dog the comfort of having you quietly nearby, connecting with your soft energy, while enjoying a tasty treat
- On the 3rd or 4th day stand up, take a few steps away from your seat then go back and sit down again.
- Each day put more distance between you, keep your energy very quiet and soft and always return to your seat.
- If your dog moves, calmly return them and the Kong to the mat without saying very much and start again.
- The aim is that you should eventually be able to go out of sight, then immediately return.
- Eventually, you should be able to carry out tasks while your dog happily chooses to relax.
- Always return to the seat and sit for a minute before removing the Kong
- Your dog should now have built up a good association with the Kong, the safe bed and learned how to drop their own

energy alongside yours and self-settle. This means you can now build up the time you leave.

For safety reasons never leave multiple dogs with food toys, unless they're separated from each other and only do this exercise with each one individually unless you have polite, reliable pooches who are 100% happy to share.

## PART 4
## EMOTIVE ENERGY BALANCING AND
## REACTIVITY

A book based on emotions would not be complete without a section on reactivity, which is perhaps one of the most intense and instinctively emotional responses our dog's experience, and something that can be positively or negatively impacted by energy transference. It is also something that seems to be on the increase in the world of pet dogs.

Whilst it's not usually something that would be classed as offensive and purposeful aggression, it can escalate if not handled appropriately and addressed, but even if it doesn't, it can be a very stressful and upsetting problem to live with on a daily basis for both you and your dog, as often the triggers that set them off are things you have to encounter in everyday life.

Reactivity is defined as 'an overreaction to an external stimulus' and these stimuli (or triggers) can be many things. Some of the most common are:

- Other dogs
- Strangers (either visiting the home or on walks)
- Men
- Children playing
- Men with beards
- People wearing glasses/hats/crash helmets
- People wearing high viz clothing
- Traffic/Motorbikes
- Bicycles / Scooters
- Large Animals
- Small Animals

In reality, a dog can be or become reactive to anything, it's totally dependent on the individual dog.

**An important note to remember: Aggressive displays are usually exhibited to avoid aggression.**

Let's look at this from the Dog's Point of View...

If you can imagine you are walking down the street, and a big strange man starts walking briskly toward you, purposefully heading straight for you. Initially, you may try to create distance and walk around him, but he moves straight into your space, so you say 'Excuse me, do you mind!' maybe raising your hand or arm in a blocking type gesture (this is your growl). If the man ignores you and continues to be in your space, you may step into him and try to push him away (this is your bark/lunge), but he hasn't taken any notice and is still in your space, maybe he even tries to touch you. Now I'm going to guess at this point (if you're anything like us) you will most likely lash out, and maybe push him or even hit him to get him away from you (this is your bite!).

Does this outburst make you an aggressive person?

Would that experience be likely to make you more afraid of strange men you see on the street? After all, he didn't actually do anything to you?

Would it make you want to avoid them?

What if you couldn't avoid them because someone had hold of your hand, and was walking you straight towards them, oblivious of how you were feeling?

What about if the man had punched you as soon as you told him to back off? Maybe next time a man started walking toward you, you wouldn't bother telling him to back off, you would just hit him first!

Can you see how that may translate for your dog? Remember, the only language and means of communicating to us how they're feeling is through body language and growling, and if we miss the first two or don't listen, the only option a dog has is to snap or bite.

The causes of reactive outbursts are often fear-based but can also be because of over-arousal, excitement or frustration but, no matter what the cause, the external behaviour is usually the same. So, whilst it can be helpful to know for teaching purposes what the cause of your dog's reactive behaviour is, from the perspective of Emotive Energy Balancing, the basic approach will follow the same set of core principles.

## So How Can Emotive Energy Balancing Help You and Your Reactive Dog?

Well given that the very core of reactive behaviour is based in emotion, there are many ways an understanding of Emotive Energy Balancing can help you. Reactivity itself is like an emotional explosion that your dog simply has no control over, they don't want to experience this any more than you want them to, they just can't help it.

Dogs that exhibit these types of behaviours generally respond well to consistency in their environment and handling, and a proactive approach from their guardian, which promotes self-control and confidence in both the canine and human halves of the partnership.

By using Emotive Energy Balancing techniques to work directly on managing energy states, alongside structured reward based teaching exercises, guardians are able to create confident, responsive habits rather than reactive ones. This, in turn, promotes consistency, and the ability to think clearly in circumstances that have previously been a blur of reactive management strategies.

By developing this ability to *respond* to a situation, rather than *react*, you as the guardian are able to remain in a naturally relaxed and positive energy state, which as we have explained can literally create a bubble of calm around you (as opposed to trying to **pretend** you're not tense or anxious, dogs know when we're pretending). Your dog can feel this energy from you and will be more likely to find it easier to connect and engage with you, trust you and have confidence in your ability to handle situations, thus promoting a reduction in reactivity.

**The Three Elements of Helping Reactive Dogs**

In order to work toward reducing reactive outbursts and help your dog to feel more comfortable in situations that currently cause them to overreact, we have found it works best to adopt a 3 pronged approach.

- Development of Protection and Trust
- Implementation of Management and Control
- Activities to Help Begin Reducing Reactivity

It's important to remember, this is not something that is suddenly going to change overnight, nor is it likely to be linear progress. You will probably find you both have good periods then not so good periods, especially if your dog has been reactive for quite some time, but the overall trend should hopefully be in a positive direction.

Not only does the energy balancing take time for **you** to master, but you also need to take into consideration that reactivity has probably become an automated 'go to' behaviour for your dog. It will take time and practise on both your parts to be able to interrupt this chain of events, be able to alter energy states, learn and implement smooth handling techniques before you can see the positive impact on behaviour and outcome.

The following protocols, we hope, should help you structure the whole process in a way that makes it easier for both you and your dog to proceed as quickly as possible.

DEVELOPMENT OF PROTECTION AND TRUST

If there is a lack of connection and trust within your relationship, and your dog doesn't feel as though when they 'speak' you listen, the scenario could be that when you're out and about on your walks, your dog feels like they're out there on their own, and therefore will take on board all the decisions that need to be made with regard to safety in this environment that is bombarding them with potential concerns.

It matters not that they may be attached to you by a piece of webbing or rope (lead), if they are not emotionally engaged with you, they could feel disconnected and the lead just becomes something they are restricted by.

What we aim to achieve with our Emotive Energy Balancing techniques alongside positive, reward based teaching methods, is to show you how to develop and strengthen your connection, so when you're out walking with your dog you are a team, but you are the decision maker in that team. Not the boss, or the leader, but the person who confidently makes the decisions that keep you both safe and comfortable in all situations, much in the same way as you would with a small child.

The bottom line is, most dogs don't want to have to make these decisions, they would love someone to take over for them so they can be relieved of that duty. Most dogs are simply not equipped with the courage and confidence needed to navigate this often scary human world, they're merely reacting out of insecurity or uncertainty.

Once we have got you back in the role of Guardian you could be amazed at how easily and happily your dog will relinquish these decisions to you.

## ACTIVITIES TO PROMOTE PROTECTION & TRUST

### Always Leave The House Calm
(Relaxed Positive Energy)

This applies to both you and your dog. If your dog can't leave the house in a calm and relaxed state, they are already up several levels on the potential to react scale before you even see any triggers.

### Settle & Engage Before You Start Your Walk
(Focus Foundation Exercise)

Take a moment outside your house to ask for a couple of behaviours to settle and focus your dog before you start your walk.  Get them connected with you and make sure they're comfortable enough to take treats right outside your house because if they're not, chances are they're already in an elevated state of alert or anxiety, and that's not setting either of you up for success.  If this is the case you might be better to continue to do the focus foundation exercise until your dog is more relaxed or choose another activity to do with them instead, to avoid having a 'bad' walk.

### Be Engaged With Your Dog During Your Walk
(Energy Transference)

Plan how you are going to have some fun together on your walk. The more time you spend engaged with your dog, the less time they are anxiously looking around for things to worry about. This also helps to build confidence for you both and strengthen the bond between you, building trust and engagement in a natural way, not just when you need to because a trigger has appeared.

### Be Present & Aware Throughout Your Walk
(Connected Energy)

Be focused on your dog throughout your walk and not distracted elsewhere.  Enjoy this time you spend together, it's your 'date' time. This will also help you **capture** great teaching moments and spot early signs of anxiety or stress build up, giving you the opportunity to **respond** calmly to those behaviours and not be left reacting to an outburst.

### Stop & Smell the Roses
(Energy/Stress Stack Management)

Rather than constantly flooding your dog with new sights, sounds and smells so they need to be checking and re-checking their environment, teach them how to hang out and chill in one spot for a few minutes.  Drop your energy, relax, help them settle their minds, have a sniff, then move on.

There's no need to ask them to sit, or down or do anything in particular, just teach them how to hang around for a moment, much the same as we would stop to enjoy the scenery so to speak. This small thing can help reduce energy and stress stacking (both of which can increase the distance to a dogs reactivity threshold) and help them to maintain a more relaxed energy state, ready to receive more environmental information.

It's also something that can become habitual and promotes the development of positive associations, so the more often your dog remains in a relaxed energy state on walks, the more often they will walk in a relaxed energy state, win-win!

NOTE: Please do choose your 'chill out' spots carefully, somewhere safe that has 360-degree vision preferably, so nothing or no one is going to sneak up on you and startle or surprise you both.

**Unwind When You Get Home**
(Energy Drop and Decompression Time)

Give your dog a gentle massage for 5 or so minutes when you return home from your walk before carrying on with your day (if this is something they would enjoy, of course, not all dogs enjoy being touched). This exercise can help both you and your dog unwind, encouraging you both to return to a more relaxed and positive energy state, especially if there were any negative experiences during your walk. It also helps to leave a more positive mental imprint on the walk experience, and help your dog to rest better, which in turn assists the body in reducing elevated stress hormones faster.

IMPLEMENTATION OF MANAGEMENT & CONTROL

As previously mentioned, because progress with this kind of emotionally driven behaviour can take time, your number one goal, to begin with, is to aim to keep your dog under threshold at all times, or as much as possible. What we mean by that is preventing your dog from being put in a position where they react.

Remember, although this may seem like you're avoiding the problem, this is, in fact, a major part of the learning process: to reduce the frequency and intensity of reactive outbursts, whilst you're working toward helping your dog feel more comfortable with these experiences.

The more times your dog reacts, the more they are practising and strengthening the behaviour of reactivity. When the other dog (or trigger) that was too close for comfort moves on by following your dog's emotional outburst, your dog will see this as a success! They don't know the dog was going to go by anyway, they think their offensive barking and lunging **made** that dog go away. So you can see why it only takes a few repetitions before this becomes their habitual 'go to' behaviour, meaning it quickly becomes a deep-seated habit.

It may help if you can think of this proactive avoidance as being a bit like driving a car. You need to know what route you're going to take before you set off and you always want to be checking what's happening around you, so you are ready to manoeuvre and respond if something unexpected occurs. A bit like in your driving test when you have to say out loud everything you see, so your instructor knows you are aware of everything happening ahead of and around you. (Do they still do that? Or are we showing our age!)

So by proactive avoidance we don't mean anxious scanning, this would create anxious energy from you, and we definitely don't want that, we just mean you want to be present and aware on your walks, so you're always in the driving seat and ready to respond calmly to any triggers that may present themselves.

This may mean any or all of the following:-

- Planning your walks so you avoid narrow paths or alleyways
- Being prepared to do a u-turn and go back the way you came, until you can find a place to gain some distance as you pass. (Sometimes it can only be those few extra feet that's needed, but it could be more depending on your particular dog's threshold)
- Crossing the street. Another reason to plan your walk carefully, if you're walking down a busy road and there's a

dog coming toward you on your side of the street, will you be able to cross the street easily?

- Nipping into someone's driveway to gain that extra few feet you need
- Always walking around the outside of bends, like with offensive driving, so you have the maximum view as you turn the corner.
- Always having an exit strategy in your mind for wherever you are walking

**Reactive Dogs Need Proactive Handling**

So these proactive avoidance strategies ideally need to happen before your dog starts reacting, don't wait to see if they're going to react or not. It's much better to **proactively respond** and create some distance as soon as you see a trigger, then if your dog remains calm, you can make good **use** of that situation as a teaching opportunity to strengthen positive associations as the trigger passes you by.

This also has the added advantage of helping you both to remain in a more relaxed energy state, feel in control and build confidence together.

If you leave your response until your dog is already reacting (over threshold) food and treats are unlikely to work anymore (emotional reactivity shuts down digestion as part of the fight or flight defence mechanism) and you're going to have to battle against them to move away from the situation. They are now in the midst of that emotional explosion, they can't help it or control it (until they are taught how to), which cannot happen from within the trigger situation.

So once your dog is in that reactivity zone, no learning or teaching can take place, all you can do is manage as best you can and get out of the situation as quickly and calmly as possible.

Once you are able to give some time and practise to change your dog's reactive emotional response to triggers, which is off topic and beyond the scope of this particular book, they will gradually be able to cope with these close encounter situations better, but until then, engagement, trust, energy state transference, proactive avoidance, management and control are your best friends.

ACTIVITIES FOR MANAGEMENT & CONTROL

**Planning Walks. Quiet Walks. No Walks?**
(Energy Stack Management)

Be aware of how your dog is feeling, and determine if a walk is the best thing for them on any given day. Of course, our dogs need exercise, and probably even more so they need the mental enrichment of leaving the confines of the house, but sometimes it's not always the best thing for them.

It may be that you are both in great energy states, feeling confident and positive, in which case an enjoyable well thought out walk would be the perfect option.

It may be that your dog has had some stressful days, which could have an impact on their reactivity threshold limit, and so it may be more beneficial for you to choose a very quiet location, where you are unlikely to come across any triggers, or if you do, you know you will have great options available for avoiding them. Open spaces, long wide tracks with lots of access or exit points should you need them, or a secure field if there is one available nearby are all great examples.

It may be that your dog finds daily walks quite stressful if you live in a built-up area and find it hard to avoid triggers, the stress build up day after day may take its toll on them emotionally. For these dogs, days off from walks can be highly beneficial.

That is not to say you should just not take them, they still need you to provide some exercise and mental enrichment, so try to find other ways to entertain them. Think of both physical and mental enrichment activities you can do together, and spend the time you would normally spend walking giving your dog some one on one attention, hanging out, bonding, relaxing and simply enjoying time together.

The games we mentioned earlier in the fun energy section may be a good place to start, and there are lots of different ways you can create enrichment activities at home. If you're stuck for ideas there is a fantastic group on Facebook called Canine Enrichment where you can find a whole array of inspiration in this area.

### Practise Exit Strategies in the Absence of Triggers
(Confident Energy Transference)

**Your** habits, behaviours and energy states have the biggest impact on your dogs - you need to practise them as much as they do. In our experience, the immediate energy state of guardians with reactive dogs, when they see another dog is instant anxiety, panic, fear and/or confusion. Imagine how this must feel to your dog in that instant? So make sure you know your management and exit strategies like the back of your hand, and practise them regularly in the absence of triggers, so they are second nature to both you and your dog.

We recommend working on just one or two exit strategies and building them up to be lovely strong habitual behaviours, so there is no confusion for you or your dog when you encounter a potentially tense situation. You can find some other areas of energy balancing we recommend to focus on with reactive dogs in Part 6.

What's great to realise is that when you are able to maintain your energy state in a trigger situation, keep things on an even keel and respond to a situation calmly and confidently with smooth and flowing behaviours, it will go a long way to helping your dog do the same.

### What to do if You See a Trigger
(Energy Match & Stream)

If you encounter a trigger situation on your walk, check your energy state instantly, change it if necessary, soften, drop, laugh, sing, skip, anything that will positively impact on your energy state, but not in a way that will startle or overwhelm your dog.

This is something you want to practise in the absence of triggers, so both you and your dog are really good at it.

Immediately aim to create distance whenever possible, even if it's only a few feet into someone's driveway. It's better to proactively create distance and then reduce it if your dog can cope, than wait to find your dog cannot cope and reacts because the trigger is too close.

- Avoid an explosion of Negative Energy shouting and getting upset yourself - this will not only add fuel to an already exploding emotional dog but could also enhance the negative associations your dog already has with the trigger.

- Avoid any form of physical punishment or aversive training method, this will most likely make your dog's reaction worse, and increase the risk of receiving a redirected bite. It could also damage your relationship with your dog, which could reduce your long term chances of eliminating the problem. A large part of rehabilitating a reactive dog lies in trust within the human-canine partnership.

- Obviously, if your dog is lunging, hold tight, but try to release the tension in the lead at any opportunity you can (See Lead Techniques in Part 5). Focus on the lead and changing your energy state, this is one of the best chances you have of impacting on your dog's behaviour in this situation.

- Try to keep yourself between your dog and the trigger. I know this is often not easy because their reactivity is usually pretty intense, hence why I recommend avoiding it as much as possible until you have done the exercises they need to be able to cope in these situations.

**Settle & Re-Connect After an Outburst**
(Drop Energy)

As soon as it is safe to do so, take at least 3 or 4 minutes to drop your energy and settle yourself and your dog before continuing on your walk.

When a dog reacts, the physiological effect is akin to a near miss when driving a car. Imagine how you feel immediately after that happens, heart racing, maybe shaking a little, legs are weak. Your dog's stress levels will have spiked and it can help prevent further reactive outbursts, and help reduce the level of stress in you if you both take at least 3-4 minutes to settle yourselves after a reaction.

Once calm you could do a few basic teaching exercises, sits, paws, high fives maybe, things they know how to do really well, to help refocus and engage with your dog in a fun way restoring confidence and positive energy before you move on.

### Three Reactive Outbursts... Go Home
(Energy / Stress Stack Management)

If you encounter three or more trigger situations that your dog reacts to on a walk, just take the quickest route home. It is likely both you and your dog will now be on a trigger stacked scale that could cause them to react to things they wouldn't normally react to. Your energy state will now most likely be pretty frazzled (technical term for anxious) and this anxious bubble around you will affect your dog, even if your lead is nice and soft. Better to just take a moment to settle and re-connect, then think about the quickest, safest route home.

Have a little teaching/playtime when you get home, if the walk was only short and if you're not both too 'stacked'. Or you could just give them a massage to help them (and you) unwind, and do something else later when you have both recovered. This would depend on how high your dog's stress levels may have become of course, they may benefit from a quiet day instead, spending quiet fun time with you.

ACTIVITIES TO HELP BEGIN REDUCING REACTIVITY

Ok, so we have established that we need to develop engagement, build trust, manage and control the environment and the situations we put our dogs into as much as possible. Whilst all of that is an essential part of the process of reducing reactivity, it is not the complete solution to changing your dog's actual emotional response to their triggers.

It is likely, however, that it will have:-

- Reduced the frequency of reactive outbursts, which is an essential part of the process.
- Reduced the intensity of the reactive outbursts and improved your dog's rate of recovery.
- Created more confidence in you, and your dog.
- Provided you both with calm, practised management and exit strategies.
- Enhanced the connection between you and your dog, and your ability to effectively communicate with them in stressful situations, which in turn will have deepened the trust and bond you have, which again, is an essential part of reducing the actual reactivity itself.

Without these foundations in place, success at reducing or eliminating the actual reactive behaviour could be much harder to achieve

### Reward All Non Reactivity in the Presence of Triggers

**IF** it's safe to do so, and at a distance your dog is comfortable with, hang out for a moment if you see a trigger, keeping the lead soft (using the lead technique as described in Part 5 of this book) whilst at the same time feeding your dog their super tasty treats as long as the trigger is in view.

If your dog would enjoy a gentle game of tug, this can also be used as a positive reward for remaining relaxed in the presence of a trigger, or even a calming bum scratch could be something your dog would find reinforcing, relaxing and rewarding in this situation (a bum scratch is, in fact, one of our dog's most rewarding activities!)

Then, after a moment, you can both move on or away from the trigger in a different direction, with both of you having remained in a relaxed, soft energy state, and with the added bonus of having had a positive experience in the presence of the trigger.

It may seem a small thing but is an essential part of the process in helping to change a dog's emotional response to triggers.

Do not underestimate the power in the simple act of you and your dog being the ones who choose to move away from the trigger situation when you are ready. Often with reactivity, a dog is rewarded for their behaviour because the trigger moves away from them, but in this scenario, you have been able to show your dog that they are safe with you, they have other choices available to them and they don't need to portray themselves as a demon dog from hell in order to make threatening things stay away from them.

This is just one way you can begin to help your dog change the emotional response they experience in the presence of triggers. Obviously there are many situations that could arise whereby you may need to do something differently, like when a loose dog runs up to your reactive dog, or you find yourself in a startle situation because of an unexpected trigger in close proximity, and whilst we would like to cover every one of those eventualities, it is impossible to do that within this particular book.

You could, however, find some great information in the recommended resource section that may provide you with more alternatives to working with your reactive dog. Many of these require structured and controlled set ups to help you and your dog learn how to handle trigger situations.

Controlled set ups are an essential part of reactivity reduction (once you both have developed your trust and foundation skills) because by taking out the element of surprise and uncertainty, this helps you both to build confidence and practise techniques for when you are on real life walks and all the unknowns that can present you both with.

Although this book is not designed to be a complete guide to rehabilitating reactive behaviour, we felt the techniques we have outlined here, together with the understanding of how Emotive Energy Balancing can help, was certainly beneficial to mention for guardians of reactive dogs, and should help to put you on a very positive path forward.

For actual techniques and activities to help reduce reactivity to triggers, and alter your dog's emotional response to these on a more permanent level, we feel the assistance of a qualified, positive reinforcement based professional trainer or behaviourist would be your best approach. We have included in our resources section at the end, details of where you can find more information on the techniques used to work with reactivity reduction on an emotional level, and the best place to locate a qualified professional who is sure to work on a positive reinforcement basis and give you all the necessary support you need.

## PART 5
## STEP BY STEP TEACHING GUIDES TO LIFESKILLS EXERCISES THAT COMPLEMENT EMOTIVE ENERGY BALANCING

Some of the following teaching guides are based on the marker method of teaching which is basically the same as clicker training except you use a marker word instead. You are welcome to use a clicker or a marker word but if you've never come across this method of teaching before, there is a more detailed explanation of how to start using it and why it's so effective in Meesh's book **Teaching Dogs Practical Life Skills**. Alternatively you could check out the video's on the **Dog's Point of View website** that will help you get started.

### VOLUNTARY CHECK IN

An exercise to build connected energy and trust on your walks. It's never too late to develop this behaviour with your dog and enhance your position as their guardian, and therefore the decision maker in the relationship. Not the boss, or the leader, just the guardian and the best person to make important decisions.

Many of our dogs can get themselves into trouble when they make their own decisions about what they do on walks. Running off to see people or other dogs, chasing things, getting themselves lost are all behaviours that are quite normal for dogs, but nonetheless ones that can be dangerous for them.

By practising and strengthening this unspoken connection between you, you should be able to enjoy more freedom with your dog, feel less stressed and more confident about situations like having them off lead (if they have a reliable recall taught of course) and feel a stronger bond with them.

- You can start this exercise at home, with just 10-15 treats at a time, and as you move around the house, each time your dog looks at you, instantly mark that look with a happy 'Yessss!' and reward them with a treat.

- We're not asking for anything so no cue word is used for this exercise, it is a choice we want our dogs to make purely on their own.
- After a day or so, start taking this exercise outside, start on lead, somewhere not too distracting, and simply mark and reward every time your dog chooses to check in with you (look at you.)
- Initially, because you are now outside with all the distracting sights, sounds and smells, your dog most likely won't check in with you to start with. You may need to be a little creative in getting those first few check ins from them, to give them the idea that the same game applies no matter where you are.
- Any of the following have shown to be good ways to elicit a quick look back from your dog, so you can mark it, reward them and continue on your way.
  - slowing down
  - stopping
  - shuffling your feet
  - sniffing
  - making a very quiet clicky noise with your tongue
- That's it! That's all you want from your dog for this exercise, to get into the habit of regularly checking in with you by choice no matter where you are.
- If your dog has a reliable recall and is allowed off lead in safe places, you can practise voluntary check in and reward them by tossing them the treat, which for some dogs really enhances the pleasure of the game, as they can either have fun catching the treat or enjoy snuffling in the grass to find it, a very enjoyable and natural behaviour most dogs find very rewarding.

**Building & Strengthening Voluntary Check In Choices**

Once your dog has got the hang of this game out on walks in low distraction areas, you want to start strengthening the behaviour, so your dog will look to you for instruction whenever they see something.

The most important part of this section of the exercise is that your dog is managed and under control, so they can't make a wrong choice. This enables you to create the ideal circumstances for them to learn the 'check in' game and win!

So this stage requires that you actively seek out all sorts of different distractions. I wouldn't recommend starting with something you know is going to send your dog into 'hyper dog land', so if you know your dog gets seriously over excited when they see another dog, leave that one until further down the list. You can of course still practise the game, if you happen to come across another dog, but try and keep your distance, this will give your dog every chance of actually being able to look away and back at you.

Make a list of things your dog finds distracting and then order them from lowest to highest level of distraction. If your dog can't look away from something at the lower level of the distraction list and be able to check in with you, they won't be able to with things at the higher end of the distraction list. By working through your list from lowest to highest, you are progressively building and strengthening the behaviour of voluntary check in, meaning it will become more reliable in everyday life.

Your list will, of course, be specific to your dog as an individual, but it may include some or all of the following:

- Strange looking objects
- People
- Children playing
- Football games
- Cyclists/scooters
- Birds
- Squirrels/Rabbits/Cats
- Other Dogs

The process of working with distractions is equally as simple

- With your dog on a lead or long line, locate a distraction that they will show interest in.
- Keep enough distance that your dog doesn't get over excited
- When your dog notices the distraction, you stop and drop your energy (Remember to say nothing)
- Wait for them to disengage (look away)  from the distraction and back at you
- Mark it (Clicker or Yesssss!) immediately raise your energy state to enhance the reward and reinforce with either food treats or a toy, maybe a tug game or gently toss a ball for them to catch (obviously the reward has to be something your dog loves, no point playing tug with a dog that doesn't like to play tug!)
- If your dog is doing great, move forward a little closer to the distraction and repeat this exercise again.  If/when your dog looks back at the distraction, stop, drop energy and wait for them to check in, mark it, raise energy, reward then move on.
- If the distraction is something your dog is allowed to have or do, like perhaps it's a dog you know and they are allowed to play with, you could use going to play with the dog as a wonderfully powerful reward for the check in. Be sure to give your dog a permission cue though, something like 'Ok Go See' or 'Go Play' so they know it's ok, otherwise they may learn to check in, but then run off thinking they're automatically allowed!
- If the distraction is something your dog is not allowed to have or do, then once they have checked in, continue to move on past the distraction, repeating the exercise as necessary. At some point, your dog should stop looking at the distraction completely, at this point give him 4-5 treats one after the other with lots of praise as you both skip away together in a wonderfully connected high energy state.

- If your dog is very distracted, i.e. they take a long time to look away and check in with you, be sure to give them a jackpot reward when they do, instant excited energy and move away from the distraction in a fun, energized way to boost the reward for them coming with you.

- Remember: You haven't ASKED them to do anything, so even though they may take a long time to make the right choice, they still made it in the end and we want to make sure they know 100% that what they did was fantastic, even though they found it hard to do.

- If your dog really struggles to disengage from the distraction, it may be that you are too close too early and your dog is not ready for this level of the game yet. Simply increase the distance and try again. As they get better at it, you can gradually reduce the distance again.

Jackpot reward = party praise, lots of treats fed quickly one after the other or if it's safe to do so you could even play a fun game of 'find it' by dribbling the treats on the ground around your dog and excitedly help them find them all. Just be careful there are no other dogs close by that might dive in and try to get the treats. Or if your dog would prefer a game with a ball or tug toy, you could use that, but really increase your fun energy and make it a super rewarding game that they will remember!

### 'IT'S OKAY'

An exercise to build awareness on your part and engagement and trust within your relationship with your dog.

Make sure with this exercise that you are only ever *responding* to your dogs behaviour and not saying 'It's Okay' because you have seen something but they haven't yet. This will have the reverse effect in that you will actually be signalling to your dog that something of concern is ahead or nearby. Your reassurance must always be in *response to their concern.*

- Start to get into the habit of saying 'It's okay' in a light confident tone consistently every time you see your dog alert to something or bark at something.

- You can start to use this at home and in the garden as well, which will help you to develop the habit and to begin building the trust and engagement connection.

- By doing this, it lets your dog know you have noticed there is something there, or even if you haven't, you have noticed that **they** have a concern about something. It lets them know you are aware and ready to deal with it if necessary, helping to build trust in you which helps with engagement and building confidence.

- In order for you to be there for your dog and develop their trust in you, you need to remain aware of them at home and on walks, so you notice when something bothers them, or when they alert to something. If you don't notice, then you can't help them, but by being proactive in these situations, immediately letting your dog know you're right there with them, it goes a long way to preventing stress stacking and anxious reactive outbursts as your dog learns that you see what they see and can help them if necessary.

- Your dog may hear something that startles them, they might see a strange object they are unsure about, or there might be an area on a walk where another dog barks at you as you go past and you can see your dog start to get anxious as you approach this spot, all these situations are great for developing your 'It's Okay' trust exercise.

- It might be that your dog simply alerts to something but you can't see what it is, this is still a great point to instantly pipe up with your 'It's Okay' to let your dog know you have spotted their concern.

- As you begin to implement this exercise, you should start to notice your dog visibly acknowledge your 'It's Okay' by shifts in their body language when you say it, indicating they have heard you, are less tense and have reconnected with you.

- Timing is quite important here, try to catch your dog **as** they alert to something but **before** they bark if you can, not easy I know and certainly to begin with will take practise.

92

Hopefully, with time and practise, you will see improvements with both the intensity of any barking or reaction and your dog's recovery time if they do react in any way to something.

- Over time, you may find your dog starts to check in with you when you say 'It's Okay' at these times, and you want to be quick to **mark** that behaviour and reward them, that will be awesome, but don't worry if they don't do it straight away, it takes time to develop trust.


## LET'S GO!

A very useful behaviour that can get you out of all sorts of situations. This is an exercise that once taught and practised can help you manoeuvre your dog easily without pushing and pulling them around. You can teach it in a really positive fun way at home, to begin with, then practise it all the time in lots of varying situations while you are out walking.

Teaching the Behaviour

- Starting at home in a very non-distracting environment
- Raise your energy and immediately begin to move away from your dog, inviting them to follow by saying 'Fido, Let's go' in a sing-song way.
- You need this to be a really positive energy exercise because when you come to use it outside it must be effective enough to compete with all the outside distractions.
- As you move away, the first few times, you could pat your leg to give your dog a visual clue as to what you want them to do
- Praise and reward as your dog follows you
- Repeat this several times each session, then end. Repeating many sessions each day will embed the behaviour more quickly in your dog's mind than if you only do it now and then.

- As soon as you can see your dog knows exactly what 'Let's Go' means and is happily trotting to catch up with you, start practising it in new ways around the home and garden.
  - Get your dog to follow you from room to room.
  - Get your dog to follow you to be given dinner.
  - Get your dog to come in from the garden with a 'let's go'
- Once your dog is doing this all the time at home, start practising it on every walk you do with them on lead and then off lead too. (if they are safe to be off lead)
- Practise periodically throughout your walk, randomly drop a 'Fido Let's go' into your walk just for the fun of it! You could go left, go right or do a U-turn.
- You can also play it as a game, by walking or running up and down the room or in the park
- You can also practise when your dog has had a really long sniff and it's time to move on
- As you turn, say 'Fido, Let's go' praise your dog for responding with a head turn to follow.
- The more fun and positive energy you put into this exercise, the more connection you can build up with your dog, meaning the behaviour will be nice and strong, making it super reliable in all sorts of circumstances.

## How Can 'Let's Go' Help in Negative Situations?

If you have a dog that has a tendency to lunge, bark or just generally become uncomfortable in certain outdoor situations, you can immediately step backwards or to the side, and say 'let's go' calmly and quietly. As your dog already knows exactly what this means, because they've had fun practising it with you, they are able to confidently respond to this cue, knowing that this is you saying 'don't worry I am going to get you out of this moment and give you the distance you're asking for'.

This also indicates to your dog that you are taking control of the situation and taking care of them, so they don't need to worry about doing it for themselves, helping them to relax and allowing you both time to take stock.

When your dog looks at you instead of the oncoming stimulant give **lots** of praise and encouragement.

As we have already mentioned, the other very good reason for teaching and practising this exercise is, if your dog reacts to something that then moves away from them, from your dog's point of view, they believe that **their** action caused the 'thing' to move away. So the embarrassing lunging, barking and sometimes screaming behaviour is accidentally reinforced and, therefore, will be repeated, because in their mind, it's a behaviour that has worked!

The more times they repeat this (and it works) the stronger and more ingrained the behaviour will come, most likely getting progressively worse.

By teaching and practising 'Let's go' in a great variety of situations and environments, you are giving your dog an alternative behaviour that is a lot more positive. Your energy will also become more relaxed as you will see other dogs, cats, squirrels, birds or distractions as an opportunity to put your method into practise. This, in turn, means that you will hopefully lose that sinking feeling that changes your energy and gives your dog a warning signal that something bad is approaching.

## LEAVE IT
### Disengage on Request

A great exercise that enables you to give a clear communication to your dog when you need them to disengage from something.

By teaching your dog to 'Leave' anything on request, you teach them to be able to disengage from environmental distractions and develop a communication that enables you to let your dog know something is unavailable to them at that time, which is super handy for those of you with dogs that like to eat unsavoury things on walks. This behaviour, once learnt, can be incredibly powerful and for us is an essential ingredient for keeping our dogs under control and safe when out walking. It enables us to allow our dogs more freedom and truly enjoy their walks, safe in the knowledge that we can prevent them from engaging in behaviours that may cause them harm or potentially place them in danger.

**Points to Remember**

- Keep your energy state relaxed but inviting throughout these exercises, some dogs can find learning how to disengage from things they want pretty hard work and if you can ensure you help them to lift their energy during these sessions, the learning process can be easier for them.

- Only very short sessions, take a break, have a play, another short session etc

- If your dog walks off, end the session, have a little game and try again a little while later. (This could be their way of saying that they are feeling a bit stressed out and need a little break)

- Never give your dog the treat/object you ask them to leave

This may seem like a lot of work, but trust us when we say, most dogs not only love learning this exercise but also progress through really quickly. It just looks a lot because we wanted to make sure we made the instructions as detailed as possible for you.

**Stage 1 - Establishing a 'Leave it' Behaviour & Adding a Cue Word**

- Using a medium value food treat, hold it in an enclosed fist in front of your dog's nose

- Allow your dog to try to get the treat from you by pushing/nibbling/licking. (No cue word yet.)

- When they give up trying to get the treat i.e. they look away, back away and stop nibbling, **click** or **mark** that **moment** and give a **high level** treat using your other hand, from a treat bag or pocket. Do not open your hand and give them the treat in your fist. *(That's a different exercise).*

- No words are necessary at this stage. You don't need to speak to your dog at all, just let them work out for themselves what they need to do.

- Repeat this for 2-3 minutes or a fixed number of times, then take a break for 5-10 minutes

- Repeat this teaching exercise a few times in quite a short space of time and you should start to notice that as soon as you offer your dog the treat, they will either back off, look away, look down or not even bother to sniff your hand, you know at this stage they have sussed it! They know in order to get a reward they must leave that treat in your hand.

- Once you know your dog is deliberately choosing to 'leave' the treat in your hand, then you can start to add your cue word. The cue word is given at the same times as you hold out the treat in your closed fist, and it would be good practise to get into the habit of always saying your dog's name followed by 'leave' or 'leave it'.

IMPORTANT NOTE: When you say your cue word, make sure you say it a normal pleasant tone of voice, with calm energy, much the same as you might say it to a child. Your dog hasn't done anything wrong, we are **asking** them to leave the treat. If you get into the habit of shouting your leave it request or saying it in a cross voice, you will not only create a repelling energy bubble around you, but you may also create a negative association for your dog around this exercise.

If that happens, it could affect how well they learn, how much they enjoy this interaction with you and so how willing they are to work with you to learn this safety exercise, all of which could ultimately affect how successful this exercise turns out to be in the real world, and we need this to be pretty spot on, it could literally save your dog's life one day.

So as you hold out the treat in your closed fist, say 'Fido Leave it' in a pleasant tone and wait for your dog to back off or stop trying to get the treat, mark it and reward with your other hand using a treat from your treat bag or pocket.

*Possible Problems*:

> If your dog doesn't even try to get your 'Leave it' food treat - use a higher level food reward (smellier, tastier) or maybe they are distracted? If so choose a quieter location or reduce any distractions.
>
> If your dog starts to get really pushy /bullying / chewing your hand - put the treat away and try using a lower value food treat, maybe just some of your dogs own food or dry biscuit.
>
> NOTE. If your dog shows any signs of becoming aggressive during this exercise, stop and contact a behaviour consultant.

YOUR GOAL FOR THIS STAGE: To issue your 'leave it' cue and have your dog leave the treat completely.

## Stage 2 - Adding an Automated Default to Guardian (Look at You)

- Remember to keep your energy state relaxed but inviting throughout these exercises

- Once your dog is really good at stage one, we can now ask for a little more from them, to explain that when we ask them to 'leave' something we actually want them to disengage from it and look to us for further instructions.

- So this time, you are going to repeat the exercise exactly the same as when you finished at stage one. Offer treat in closed fist > 'Fido Leave it' > but now you are going to withhold the click or marker until your dog actually looks up at your face.

- Most dogs, when the click or 'Yessss!' marker doesn't come as they expected, will look at you as if to say 'hey where's my click?' and THAT is your new 'CLICK POINT' lots of praise, smile! (Great Energy Transmitter) and reward as before, with your higher value treat from your treat bag or pocket.

***Possible Problem***: If your dog doesn't look up at your face when you withhold the click

> Make sure your energy is nice and inviting and your face soft and smiling (we can sometimes look a bit intense when we are teaching, and this can give off a harsh energy)

> Give your dog a clue - Make a very slight squeak or sniff or kissy noise, move your head slightly into their eye line and they will normally look, then you can click/mark, praise and reward

> Repeat with your clue another 2 or 3 times, then see if they can do it without the clue

> Be prepared to WAIT for your dog to work things out, don't be too hasty in assuming they're not going to do it. Just sit and wait for quite a few seconds and see what happens, you'll be amazed at how quick they can problem solve when we don't interfere!

Most dogs cotton on to this very quickly, some dogs, however, can find looking directly at our face uncomfortable. If this is the case with your dog, you can mark and reward for glances in your general face direction, you can also make sure your head is turned slightly away from them, making it more comfortable for them to look at you.

Repeat the exercise with plenty of short sessions until your dog is doing this really well before moving on to the next stage.

YOUR GOAL FOR THIS STAGE: To give your 'Fido leave it' request and have your dog ignore the treat and look at you.

### Stage 3 - Strengthening the New Behaviour & Generalising to All Locations

Once you know your dog understands stage 2 of the game and is reliably looking away from your hand and back to your face following your 'leave it' request start to practise in different locations.

- practise this in different rooms of the house
- practise it with distractions in the house - people in the room/things going on
- practise it out in your garden
- practise it out on a walk (a very familiar walk where your dog won't be too distracted)
- practise it out on a busy walk with more distractions

### Stage 4 - Transferring the Behaviour to Floor Based Items

- Now the next stage is to place your hand on the floor with 'leave it' treat underneath it
- As you put your hand down, say your dog's name and give your 'leave it' cue (in a pleasant tone)
- As before, wait for your dog to back off your hand and look at you - then mark and treat from your pocket or treat bag
- Most dogs understand the game pretty well by now, and cotton on quickly, but if they take a while to start with, because we've changed the game a little bit, you can give them a little clue the first couple of times, by making a little sniffy noise to get that look up to you.
- Once your dog is doing well with that part of the exercise, you can slowly start to uncover the treat on the floor, and give your 'leave it' request, but remain with your hand close by to cover it again if they try to grab it!
- Repeat 3 or 4 times then take a break, remember to pick up your 'leave it' treat from the floor as you finish each session
- By taking regular breaks, it gives you the opportunity to put the 'leave it' treat down in a new place each time, helping to generalise the behaviour for your dog.
- Repeat these sessions until you can place a treat on the floor > say 'Fido leave it' > and your dog will immediately look to you without attempting to get the treat on the floor.
- Once your dog can do this, place the treat on the floor, give your 'leave it' request and stand up

- If your dog tries to take the treat cover it with your foot
- Wait until they look up at you - mark, praise and treat from your pocket or treat bag
- Don't allow your dog to take the treat from the floor, although sometimes they're super quick and it happens by accident, but don't worry, just reset and start again, or maybe start with the treat under your foot, and then you can uncover it as you say 'leave it'
- Repeat this exercise in various rooms around the house
- Repeat this exercise with a variety of treats - always rewarding with something higher value than what is being left.
- Remember to say your dog's name before your cue and to give the 'leave it' request only once and wait for your dog to respond, the more he works things out for himself without prompting, the stronger the behaviour should be.
- Also remember, your dog is never allowed to get the 'leave it' item. When you have finished a session pick it up and remove it
- When your dog is working well with this, practise with lots of different objects, starting with low interest objects and working up to more interesting ones.
- Once your dog is reliable at home and in the garden, start working on and practising the exercise out on your walks using objects you take with you (you can randomly drop them on the floor then come across them) or use objects you come across on your walk that your dog shows interest in.

YOUR GOAL FOR THIS STAGE: To be able to place a desirable treat or object on the floor and have your dog ignore it and look at you instead, both at home and on walks.

### SETTLE
Self-Relaxation & De-Compression Time

This is an essential exercise for teaching your dog to learn how to switch off, relax and be calm. It is particularly useful for anxious dogs who feel the need to follow you everywhere and can tend to worry about all sorts of little everyday things in life.

There are two ways to teach self-relaxation. The first is free shaping and the second is a more structured teaching approach, but we will cover them both for you here

### SETTLE - Free shaping teaching method

- So to begin, every time your dog is laying down relaxed and happy (but not sleeping!) and **not** focused on you, reward them with a treat between their paws and say 'good job, well done.'
- If they are sitting or laying and staring at you, this doesn't count, because they are still focused on you and expecting something. It's understandable that you may not want to speak to them, or disturb them, as you feel beyond relieved that you finally have some peace but trust us, this will eventually result in more peace for you both, not less.
- At first, they may instantly fly at you happily, thinking this is an invitation to interact and if they do this, then for the purpose of this self-relaxation exercise, simply ignore their attempts to take you out like a four-legged ninja!.... and go about what you were doing.
- Wait for them to settle again then praise softly and lay a few treats at their paws
- Build up to the point where you can chat to them softly without them needing to charge at you.
- If your dog remains relaxed and laid down, reward them again, then walk away and go about what you were doing,
- Continue this gradually increasing the amount of time in between laying treats at their paws
- When they're really good at remaining relaxed and settled, you could start to walk out of the room and straight back in again, rewarding with a treat for staying laid down and settled.

- Keep practising this exercise at appropriate times, until your dog realises that it's ok to relax and to be by themselves, that you will not suddenly escape from the house without them noticing, or that the only time they get your attention is when they're asking for it, or following you everywhere.

## SETTLE - Structured teaching method

The second way to teach self-relaxation is a more structured approach, and this exercise will work best if you can choose carefully the time of day you teach it to begin with. Most of us know what times of day our dogs are calmer than others, so avoid choosing a time when your dog may be overexcited, this would make it harder for them to do and thus slow down the learning process. I would also recommend avoiding a time when your dog is tired or visibly stressed, none of us learns well when we're tired or stressed, do we?

Once learnt, this exercise can be used to ask your dog to settle at times when they may be a bit over excited, but during the learning stages, in order to set them up for success, we want them to be in a 'ready to settle energy state'

- Begin indoors, in a quiet room with no distractions. Have your dog with a simple flat collar on and a 6ft lead if you think they will be distracted and wander off or mob you for treats or attention.

- Have a store of treats to hand, in your pocket or in a treat bag/pot next to you. This exercise will probably work best if you have treats your dog likes and so will find reinforcing, but not so high value that they get all overexcited about them.

- Holding the end of the lead, take a seat in a chair, drop your energy and relax. You could have a book or magazine to hand to imitate reading, or you could simply sit and look out the window. The point here is not to sit staring at your dog, we want them to notice your energy drop which should transfer to them indicating nothing is going to be happening. For some dogs, if you sit and look at them, they won't settle down but will instead view this as a teaching situation and could start offering all sorts of behaviours or may even start to get frustrated.

- There is no cue here, you don't need to say anything, just relax. As you disengage, remain aware of what your dog is doing - most dogs, if you have timed this right, will fairly quickly just lay down at your feet. As soon as they do this, take a treat and calmly place it between their paws.

- You don't need to say anything, praise them or touch them, just place the treat and sit back again.

- At this point your dog may instantly get up, that's fine, just remain relaxed, disengaged and wait for them to settle again, repeating as above.

- If your dog remains laying down, count slowly to 5 and then place another treat between their paws. Again say nothing, remain in low energy state, place the treat and sit back.

- If your dog remains laying down but is staring at you, waiting for the next treat, try to wait until they break that stare, then instantly (but calmly) place another treat between their paws without engaging in eye contact or praising.

- If your dog continues to lay in his relaxed position, without constantly staring at you, continue counting to 5 and placing a treat in the same way.

- Repeat this for two minutes, no longer, then look at your dog, praise them and stroke them calmly, get up and move to another spot and repeat the exercise for another 2 minute, or end there. You can build up the length of time your dog will remain settled later on, after they understand the exercise completely.

-  If your dog looks tired, end the session and do another one later in the day when they are calm.

- If your dog drops into a very relaxed state i.e. they look soft in their face and body, they have flopped their bottom to the side in a relaxed position and maybe even laid their head down, you could choose to place a treat, unclip the lead and walk quietly away.

- When you end this exercise, whether your dog is completely relaxed or not, end it calmly. Remain in your low energy state, smile in their direction, say in a whisper 'good settle' and quietly walk away. Avoid ending the session by giving excited praise or tickles as this is going to immediately raise their energy state and undo all the calmness of the session.

***Possible problem***: your dog may not settle at all, may repeatedly try to climb on you or get the food

Have lower value treats

Try a different time of day

Mark & reward any and all small signs of relaxation, break the chain down into smaller steps. Things such as a softer body, a look away or a sit - but always place the food quietly on the floor between your dog's paws without engaging with them, sit back and relax. You should gradually be able to build up to higher levels of relaxation with each session and more practise.

### Building up Duration and Adding Distractions

Once your dog can settle well in different positions around your home when it's quiet, you can start to increase the time they will spend in settle and also begin adding gradual distractions.

Make sure you start with low level distractions and build up to things your dog finds particularly distracting, otherwise you won't be setting them up to succeed.

Always work on length of time and distractions separately. So if you are building up the time they will stay settled, do it with no distractions. If you are adding distractions, reduce the amount of time you expect them to stay settled.

### LEAD TECHNIQUES
Maintaining soft energy on walks.

One of the most important aspects of being able to maintain soft energy between you and your dog on your walks is being able to release any tension in the lead. It takes two to pull, and your dog is not going to be the one to stop because of opposition reflex. All that means is, whenever they feel pressure against their bodies, in this case, their necks or chests, they automatically respond by leaning against it, this behaviour is a reflex action and can be both self-rewarding and stress inducing.

If you are pulling against your dogs pulling, or even trying to hold them at the end of the lead, they are going to find it very difficult to stop leaning against you, so this technique should help you learn how to quickly break that pulling cycle.

LEAD STROKING

Lead stroking is a calming technique we learnt from the Tellington TTouch method of working with dogs. It complements our Emotive Energy Balancing work perfectly.

The technique for lead stroking is pretty much what it says on the tin

- Make sure you drop and soften your energy - practise being able to do this quickly, it can be really helpful in so many situations where we have a tendency to become anxious or tense.
- As your dog stands leaning at the end of the lead: one hand will be on the handle of the lead, and place your other further along the lead and begin gently but firmly sliding this hand back and forth along the lead.
- This helps transmit your soft energy down the lead and creates a gentle vibration which helps release the tension of the pulling cycle for you both.
- As you do this, you should see and feel your dog begin to calm and the tension reduce (less pulling).
- When this happens, relax the hand holding the handle of the lead (but keep hold of the handle) and use this hand to stroke the lead as well, in a hand over hand type movement, taking each hand forward and stroking back toward you along the lead.

- Your dog should have stopped pulling against you at this point because you have released all the tension in the lead, giving them nothing to pull against.
- You can regain their attention, reposition or move away depending on the situation you're in.

LEAD WALKING

This is a really handy technique that enables you to get closer to your dog, but without pulling on them and creating tension in the lead. For example, you're walking along a track, your dog relaxed at the end of their lead or long line, and your dog alerts to something, maybe a dog or a small furry animal. Although they haven't reacted yet, you know they might and want to be closer to them so they can't launch themselves forward and so you have greater control over manoeuvring them away if necessary. If you just pull on the lead to get them back, you increase the risk of *causing* a reaction and you create tension in the lead that is likely to cause them to pull against you.

- Let's say you have the handle of the lead in your left hand, as your dog alerts to something immediately place your right hand onto the lead, a bit further along from where you're holding the handle.
- Keeping hold of the handle, place your left hand further along in front of your right hand, so you're walking hand over hand down the lead.
- Repeat this hand over hand action, folding up the lead with each hand as you go, until you're right next to your dog with them on a nice short manageable length lead. Be aware at this point that you're not pulling or tightening the lead.
- You're now in a position to regain their attention and either simply connect with them as you both watch the distraction move away, or you can give them further instructions to 'Let's go' or 'Sit'. The likelihood of them being able to respond has increased, because you're now close beside them, and they know that you're also aware of the distraction.

## PART 6
## HOW EMOTIVE ENERGY BALANCING CAN BE APPLIED TO SOME COMMON TRAINING & BEHAVIOUR ISSUES

In this section, we wanted to try to give you a simple guide to what key areas to focus on in relation to some of the most common problems we encounter when working with our clients. That way you can go back to each of those sections in the book and apply them individually to your particular situation.

### Walking on a Loose Lead

- Visualisation
- Energy Drop
- Energy Stack Management - set yourself up to succeed by teaching exercises before adding to the stack (i.e. more people/dogs)
- Focus Foundation
- Lead techniques
- Positive energy bubble
- Self-awareness - How is your behaviour and energy having a positive or negative effect on your dogs

It's important to remember when working on loose lead walking exercises that you can literally repel your dog with your energy bubble making it very hard for them to feel comfortable and **want** to walk by your side. By the same token you can use your energy to attract them to walk beside you with an energy bubble that is positive, inviting and engaging. Remember those people you meet who you just feel drawn to and just being around them feels good, those people have positive energy bubbles that are inviting and highly contagious.

## Jumping Up

- Energy Stack Management
- Energy drop
- Energy bubble
- Positive brain focus - Focus on what you want your dog to do instead of what you want them to stop doing.
- Self-awareness - How is your behaviour and energy having a positive or negative effect on your dogs

The key areas for working with a dog that likes to leap all over everyone is making sure their learning environment starts at the lowest level of distraction and progresses gradually. If they haven't yet learnt not to jump up at very familiar people it's unfair to expect them to be able to do it with exciting strangers and visitors. The second key area is self-awareness, we often see people who are unaware of how *their* behaviour is reinforcing their dog for jumping up.

## Barking

- Energy matching & streaming
- Positive brain focus - Teach your dog alternative behaviours incompatible with barking.
- Energy Bubble
- Energy Stack Management
- Self-awareness - How is your behaviour and energy having a positive or negative effect on your dogs

Although barking is a completely natural form of communication for dogs and it's unrealistic to expect them not to do it at all, we do appreciate that some dogs can be real chatterboxes! When working to reduce the level or intensity of your dogs barking, it's important to be aware of how **you** are responding to it (make sure you're not joining in) and also to address what is driving the behaviour. If your dog is barking excessively because they're anxious or bored, teaching an alternative incompatible behaviour is unlikely to be successful without first addressing those emotional needs.

## Recall

- Energy Matching & Streaming
- Energy bubble
- Bonding energy circle
- Fun energy
- Own your space
- Visualisation
- Self-awareness - How is your behaviour and energy having a positive or negative effect on your dogs

Emotional energy is a real biggie when working on recall exercises, anxious, frustrated or angry energy can make it really difficult for your dog to *want* to return to you. We fully appreciate how frustrating it can be when you're in a situation and you *need* your dog to come back to you, but in that instance we urge you to check your energy and try to instantly shift into a positive, fun or excitable energy state to help attract your dog towards you.

This is of course something best practised when not in a 'situation' so make sure you get lots of positive energy ploughed into your recall exercises whenever you're working on them. Be the kind of person **you** would love to hang out with and hopefully your dog will develop the same feeling.

## Hyperactivity

- Energy Stack Management
- Energy drop
- Positive brain focus
- Energy matching & streaming
- Settle & Decompression time

- Self-awareness - How is your behaviour and energy having a positive or negative effect on your dogs

The key areas for dealing with hyperactive canines are energy stack management and helping them learn how to truly relax and decompress. Some dogs are more prone to hyperactivity than others and it would be helpful for you to be aware of what things amp your dog up so you can counteract them with other activities that will help restore them to a lower level energy state making it easier for them to switch off.

### Fear of People or Dogs (Reactivity)

- Energy drop
- 'It's Okay'
- Energy stack management
- Decompression time
- Visualisation
- Self-awareness - How is your behaviour and energy having a positive or negative effect on your dogs

In the first instance we would recommend you locate a suitably qualified professional to help you get started working with a dog that shows fearful behaviours towards people or dogs. It's such a powerful emotionally driven behaviour it can be all too easy to make mistakes that could cause more problems than it solves.

A qualified professional will help you recognise all the signals and communications you need to be aware of in the way your particular dog presents them, so you will be able to help them in the best and most effective way possible.

### Fear of Objects

- 'It's Okay'
- Energy drop
- Energy stack management

- Decompression time
- Self-awareness - How is your behaviour having a positive or negative effect on your dogs

When working with a dog that displays fearful behaviours of new or strange objects your energy can be a very helpful support strategy.

This together with providing appropriate environmental management and support through distance creation and being able to recognise the difference between the times when they need your help, and when it's ok to allow them to assess something for themselves and develop their own confidence in doing so.

### Boundary Guarding

- 'It's Okay'
- Energy matching & streaming
- Visualisation - to help you control your energy projection.
- Focus foundation
- Enrichment - make sure boredom isn't a contributing factor.
- Energy stack management
- Self-awareness - How is your behaviour and energy having a positive or negative effect on your dogs

Boundary guarding is always a tricky one because on the one hand we would probably quite like our dogs to alert us to things in or near our home that may be a cause for concern, but at the same time we would rather they weren't constantly shouting down the neighbourhood. This is another one where energy can have a profound effect in both a positive or negative way. It's about the repetition of exercises that will help your dog learn that you are grateful to them for alerting you to a potential danger, but when you have checked and told them 'It's Okay' they need to learn to stand down and let it go.

# PART 7
# OTHER ENERGY RELATED TECHNIQUES

We just wanted to mention here some other techniques that complement Emotive Energy Balancing and could enhance your dog's health, lifestyle, physical and mental wellbeing.

## Reiki

Reiki is a Japanese technique for stress reduction and relaxation that also promotes healing. It is administered by "laying on hands" and is based on the idea that an unseen "life force energy" flows through us and is what causes us to be alive. If one's "life force energy" is low, then we are more likely to get sick or feel stress, and if it is high, we are more capable of being happy and healthy.

The word Reiki is made of two Japanese words - Rei which means "God's Wisdom or the Higher Power" and Ki which is "life force energy". So Reiki is actually "spiritually guided life force energy." A treatment feels like a wonderful glowing radiance that flows through and around you. Reiki treats the whole person or animal including body, emotions, mind and spirit creating many beneficial effects that include relaxation and feelings of peace, security and wellbeing.

Reiki is a simple, natural and safe method of spiritual healing and self-improvement that can be effective for both humans and animals. It also works in conjunction with all other medical or therapeutic techniques to relieve side effects and promote recovery.

## TTouch

Tellington Touch or TTouch is a specialised approach to the care and teaching of animals developed by internationally recognised animal expert, Linda Tellington-Jones PhD (Hon). This method, based on cooperation and respect, offers a positive approach to teaching animals and can improve health, promote calm and present solutions to common behavioural and physical problems. It helps establish a deeper rapport between humans and their animals through increased understanding and more effective communication.

Using a combination of specific touches, lifts and movement exercises, TTouch helps to release tension and increase body awareness. This can help animals cope with being handled without provoking typical fear responses. You can also help an animal develop self-confidence in previously frightening situations by using TTouch alongside a variety of other tools. It can also be used to assist with recovery from illness or injury, or just simply to enhance quality of life and the bond between you and your animals.

**Massage**

Canine Massage is a holistic, hands-on therapy that promotes health in dogs, the benefits of which may include relaxation, increased oxygenation, relief from pain, improved joint flexibility, as well as a variety of benefits to the immune system.

'Holistic' means that the whole body is treated rather than just the injured spot. Often there can be referred pain from the primary area of an injury to another part of the body – the secondary area. For example, if your dog is limping on his right front leg, he may compensate by putting extra strain on the left lower back muscles.

Touch is vital for humans and animals – soft, soothing strokes warm and relax muscles and can help to create calm energy and aid learning. It is thought that by encouraging a dog to fully relax following a walk and/or teaching session improves the brain's ability to process and absorb information.

# CLOSING WORDS

We really hope that you have enjoyed reading and learning about Emotive Energy Balancing, how it affects both you and your four-pawed family members, and how the application of this knowledge alongside positive reinforcement teaching methods can help to improve your dog's behaviours, responses and emotional well being.

As science and research continues in the world of dogs there are more and more people becoming aware that dogs are simply not 'just dogs'. Their intelligence and capacity for learning alongside their emotional responses and reactions are both simple and complex at the same time, and it this paradigm that is most fascinating.

For us, what is even more fascinating, is that we can have such a hugely positive impact on not only our dog's energy but also our own in the process. By learning and understanding how to change energy states, both yours and your dogs, we are able to create a more positive mindset, develop more confidence and feel empowered that we don't have to be a slave to our emotional energy, and that with our help, our dogs don't have to be either.

We hope you will join our **Facebook group** and share your experiences of Emotive Energy Balancing with us. We know our learning will never end, and we are excited to continue working toward even more understanding, better ways to communicate and the deepest symbiotic relationship that can be possible between species. We owe it to ourselves, and we owe it to our dogs.

If you have enjoyed this book and feel the concepts we have discussed here would be beneficial to other people who choose to share their lives with canine companions, why not help them by leaving a review for the book on Amazon so they will be aware of what they could gain from learning about and understanding how to incorporate Emotive Energy Balancing into their everyday lives and interactions with their own dogs.

# ABOUT THE AUTHORS

**Janeen Warman**

Janeen is business owner at **Human Hound Healing** and has been working with dogs and their people for over 20yrs. 4yrs ago, whilst running classes at a local day care facility, she was finding it difficult to settle into the class teaching environment, because of the issues she could see happening, but was only able to offer limited help because of the time restrictions of the group situation. This was reinforced when out walking on the beach one evening, just as it was getting dark, suddenly hearing shouts of 'sorry!' shortly followed by a bounding dog, being chased by harassed looking owners. After chatting to them and quite a few others like them, she found they were ashamed to go to classes, they were even too embarrassed to go out in daylight with their dogs. She knew these were the people that needed to be reached, and they needed something more than just 'dog training'. This was when she changed both the way she worked with clients and the business name to Human Hound Healing.

It was also around this time that Janeen got involved in helping to rehabilitate Romanian street dogs, and how she came to meet her co-author on this project Meesh Masters. They instantly connected and became firm friends, and it was then that a torch was lit. Following hours and hours of talking and researching over the last 2 years, Emotive Energy Balancing grew. It was already within the work they were both doing with their human and canine clients, they just needed to be able to explain it in words, teach it and share it as a valuable accompaniment to their positive, reward based teaching methods and techniques.

Janeen has studied the Canine Human Interface, has diplomas in Canine and Animal Psychology, completed numerous courses with Dr Ian Dunbar, Sarah Whitehead and is a Reiki Master with Reiki Animal Practise Certification. She currently lives in Southern England with her 2 children and 3 dogs.

**Meesh Masters**

Meesh is business owner at **The Dog's Point of View** and has enjoyed the great privilege of being guardian to many dogs over the last 30 years, and worked with all breeds and sizes with her clients over the last 15 years. She has a passion for not only canine psychology but also human psychology and how the two are intertwined. Her journey as a trainer started around 20 years ago when she needed help with a GSD rescue dog with some quite extreme behavioural problems. After paying a lot of money to enlist the help of a behaviourist, was dismayed to find their approach was one of force and a lack of empathy for the emotional wellbeing of her struggling dog. After asking them to leave, she started reading everything she could find in an attempt to try to help her dog herself and thus began taking courses and studying. She hasn't stopped reading yet...

After becoming involved with Romanian rescue dogs two years ago, both as a support advisor to new adopters and a fosterer, she was once again led to look deeper into the thinking, feeling, emotional depths of the dogs we spend our lives with. After realising how the Romanian dogs were different to British born dogs, how their genetics and bloodline, being from street dogs meant they seemed to be more in tune with their instinctive natures and noticing how much this affected their response to 'training' in the conventional sense at times, she found she was working with them in a completely different way. As she began to apply the same approach with all of her other clients, it became very evident that this way of teaching was not only more successful but easier for both clients and their dogs to relate to.

After getting to know, and having an instant affinity with Janeen through their work together with the Romanian rescue dogs, they found they were doing the same things with their clients, but there was no 'teaching' explanation for it. Hence Emotive Energy Balancing was born.

Meesh has diplomas in Advanced Canine Psychology and training and a diploma in Life Coaching. She has also completed numerous courses with Dr Ian Dunbar, is a Reiki

Master with Animal Reiki Certification and is a Member of the Pet Professional Guild British Isles. She currently lives in South Yorkshire with her Border Collie and Romanian rescue dog.

**Interesting Fact**

As this book comes to completion, we thought it might be an interesting fact to share with you that, as of yet, even though we have researched and written this book together, we have never actually met in person! We hope to be rectifying that very soon.

# TEACHING DOGS PRACTICAL LIFE SKILLS

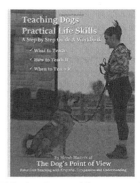

We wanted to point out and direct you to a book already available on Amazon called Teaching Dogs Practical Life Skills - A Step by Step Guide & Workbook which was published last year by Meesh Masters.

Our book on Emotive Energy Balancing complements perfectly the information and techniques detailed in the Life Skills book. This book provides you with the more science based practical and technical exercises that you can teach your dogs to help you solve a whole range of teaching and behaviour challenges.

By using the information from both books, you are not only provided with the science-based techniques and knowledge that will help you teach your dog, but also the deeper understanding that comes with energy awareness and how important it is to include both within your day to day interactions for that in tune, flowing relationship that appears as if both you and your dog have an unspoken language between you.

# RECOMMENDED RESOURCES & FURTHER INFORMATION

## Reactivity Resources

BAT (Behaviour Adjustment Training) - Grisha Stewart
http://www.grishastewart.com/

C.A.R.E for Reactive Dogs - www.careforreactivedogs.com

LAT Training - Leslie McDevitt - www.controlunleashed.net

Reactive Dog Owners Group on Facebook
www.facebook.com/groups/1633448230248202

Secure Dog Walking Fields Directory
www.dogwalkingfields.co.uk

## Positive Reward Based Professional Dog Trainers: Recommended Membership Bodies

PPG - The Pet Professional Guild
www.petprofessionalguild.com

PPGBI - The Pet Professional Guild British Isles
www.petprofessionalguild.co.uk

IMDT - The Institute of Modern Dog Trainers
www.imdt.uk.com

PPN - The Pet Professional Network
www.petpronetwork.com

ISCP - The International School of Canine Practitioners
www.theiscp.com

COAPE - Centre of Applied Pet Ethology
www.coape.org

VSPDT - Victoria Stilwell Positively Dog Training
www.positively.com

KPACTP - Karen Pryor Academy Certified Training Partner
karenpryoracademy.com

APBC - Association of Pet Behaviour Counsellors
www.apbc.org.uk

APDT - Association of Pet Dog Trainers
www.apdt.co.uk

## REFERENCES

Elaine Hatfield - Emotional Contagion - Published 1994
http://www.elainehatfield.com/uploads/3/4/5/2/34523593/46.
_hatfield_cacioppo__rapson_1992.pdf

http://www.elainehatfield.com/uploads/3/4/5/2/34523593/50.
_hatfield_cacioppo__rapson_1993.pdf

Hatfield, E., & Rapson, R. L. (1998). Emotional contagion
and the communication of emotion. In M. T. Palmer & G. A.
Barnett (Eds.), Progress in Communication Sciences, 14, 73-
89.

William Campbell / Dr Ian Dunbar - Jolly Routine -
https://www.amazon.co.uk/Behavior-Problems-Dogs-W-
Campbell/dp/0966870506

Nando Brown - School of Canine Science -
https://www.youtube.com/user/InTheDoghouseDTC

Victoria Stillwell - Inside Your Dog's Mind -
https://www.udemy.com/insideyourdogsmind/

Doggone Safe - Be A Tree Programme -
https://vimeo.com/210452016

Tellington TTouch - Linda Tellington Jones -
http://www.ttouch.com/

Amy Cuddy (Social Psychologist) - 2012-Ted Conference -
Power Position -
https://www.youtube.com/watch?v=DHuUKGRQEk0

Printed in Great Britain
by Amazon